I0832457

THE TOMORROWS I ALMOST LOST

Post-Traumatic Growth for Warriors, First Responders, and the Silent Half of Every Uniform

Chris "Elroy" Stricklin

USAF Colonel (Ret.)

THE TOMORROWS I ALMOST LOST

Post-Traumatic Growth for Warriors, First Responders, and the Silent Half of Every Uniform

ISBN-13: 979-8-9961763-0-4 (Paperback)

This book is a memoir. The author's own events, including the ejection of September 14, 2003, are drawn from personal experience and from Air Force records. Passages reflecting the author's work alongside veterans, first responders, and their families appear with identifying details removed; some accounts are composites. Conversations have been reconstructed from memory. The stories shared here appear in the spirit in which they were entrusted—to help someone else find their way.

This book is not intended as a substitute for medical, psychological, or therapeutic treatment. Readers should consult qualified professionals for any matters relating to physical or mental health. If you or someone you know is in crisis, please contact the Veterans Crisis Line by dialing 988 and pressing 1, or text 838255. You can also reach the 988 Suicide & Crisis Lifeline by calling or texting 988.

Published by Military Mentorship Mastermind

All profits donated to Warrior Retreat, an initiative of the Alabama Veteran Initiative.

First Edition: 2026

Printed in the United States of America

Yesterday shaped you.

Today defines you.

Tomorrow is yours to build.

CONTENTS

✦

All profits donated to Warrior Retreat, an initiative of the Alabama Veteran Initiative.

PREFACE

I should have died.

That sentence isn't dramatic. It is a precise description of something real. Doctors, after the fact, told me one after another the science of my body coming home that day didn't add up. Engineers, after the fact, told me the math of my ejection didn't add up. The science and math are what they are. I am still here.

On September 14, 2003, in Mountain Home, Idaho, I ejected from an F-16 60 feet above the ground, ½ second before ground impact, outside the survivable envelope of the ejection seat. From the ground, the team saw what they saw. From the air, the commander saw what he saw. They concluded what every set of eyes on the field had concluded.

They called my wife. She heard I was dead. Terri took that call before she got the one that said I was alive. I want you to sit with that for a moment. There was a window of time, narrow but real, when the woman I had grown up with, my high school sweetheart, the mother of our children, the silent half of my uniform, knew only that her husband was gone. She lived inside that window before she lived inside the correction. I have spent the years since trying to make up for that window.

The years between that day and this page have been long. They have not been wasted. What grew in me during those years has a name now. The research calls it post-traumatic growth. I call it survivor's obligation.

Survivor's obligation is a calling to make the tomorrows I almost lost intentional. It is the vulnerability and discipline of taking my family's darkest day and turning it into something other people can learn from, grow through, and heal alongside. It is the choice I make every morning, walking out onto a porch in Alabama to a sunrise I almost did not live to see.

I am writing this book because that obligation has not been mine to carry alone. For years now, I have volunteered with veteran missions that work with the mental, emotional, and spiritual struggles of life after trauma and stood next to men and women who carry stories the official paperwork never accounted for. Somewhere along the way, people started trusting me with their struggles and opened with sentences they had never spoken before.

I have never told anybody this.

I am struggling.

I am not OK.

Every time those sentences arrive, I understand more clearly what kind of work this is. It is the work of being present when someone has nowhere else to put what they are carrying. To carry someone else's story is an honor I do not take lightly. This book is the consolidation of my own story and the stories of those who have trusted me with theirs.

I am writing for every veteran who once wrote a check payable to the United States of America for an amount up to and including their life, and who quietly hoped the check would not be cashed. I am writing for the man or woman who never wore the uniform but lived next to it. Who paid the bill, raised the children, and held the family together while the focus stayed on the one in the photograph. I am writing for the first responder who walks into the rooms most people will spend their lives walking past and walks home carrying what they saw.

If that is you, I see you.

If that is somebody you love, I see them too.

What this book is, more than anything else, is the right questions in the right order. The questions that helped me out of my own slow sinking. The questions that brought Terri and me back into the same conversation after thirteen years of not having it. The questions that helped men I love begin to tell their own families the things that had been waiting in private for decades. I don't have the answers. Asking the questions with care is how the door opens.

Let me say what this book isn't. It isn't an answer, and it isn't a clinical guide. It's not a sermon nor the thing that will fix you. Nothing in you needs fixing in that way. Something in you might need translating, and we'll come back to that.

If you came to this book carrying something heavy, I'm not waiting on the other side of your story with a finish line. I'm somewhere in the middle of mine. I have been at this work a little longer than you have, and I have made a lot of mistakes you don't have to repeat. That's all. I was blessed to wake again this morning. I am still living the tomorrows I almost lost.

If you need a hand, mine is here.

A LETTER TO THE READER

There comes a point when suffering stops feeling like an interruption to your life and starts becoming the wallpaper of it. You stop noticing it the way you stop noticing a sound that's been running for years. To everyone watching, you appear capable, even formidable, someone who has weathered things and come out reinforced. What they don't see is the slow erosion underneath. The resilience they admire is mostly choreography. The daily work of arranging your face into something that can pass.

The mind, when it turns on itself, doesn't always do so with violence. Sometimes it just debates. Endless rooms of arguments where every voice is a version of you, and the ruling never comes. Sleep becomes negotiable. Food becomes optional. There are hours that don't appear on the official clock. Hours spent attending to injuries that rest in places no bandage can find.

For warriors, what people call breakdown often takes the form of composure. The most dismantled among us are frequently the ones who arrive on time, return the call, perform capability with such fluency that even we begin to confuse the performance for the truth. Inside, something keeps dying quietly, without ceremony, a funeral no one is ever invited to.

This is not a confession written for sympathy. There is someone reading these pages whose interior matches them too closely to be coincidence; Someone carrying the same uninvited weight, rehearsing the same composure, fluent in the same private grammar of laughing through the dark. You are the reason I'm writing it down. If I am here, intact enough to put words to this, then proof exists that remaining is possible. Take it. Borrow my evidence until you have your own.

The pages that follow come from the heart. Mine, and the hearts of the veterans and first responders who have trusted me with theirs. The intention is not to lecture. It is to start a conversation among people who already understand the shape of this. We are out here. Everywhere. In every uniform, every quiet house, every shift change, every empty hour after midnight. You are not making this walk alone. There are others whose interior matches yours and we stand together in support and love. Know that you are seen. Know that you are heard.

CHAPTER 1

COMING HOME TO YOURSELF

Somewhere along the way, I stopped telling my story from a place of pain. The pain didn't go anywhere. It still lingers and rearranges the furniture when I'm not looking. Some nights it sits at the foot of the bed. Some nights it sits on my chest making it hard to breathe. I just stopped telling the story from inside the wound.

For a long time, everything I'd been through felt like something I was supposed to recover from. There was a version of me sitting on the other side of all of it, the version before the ejection, before the deployments, before the friends who didn't come home, before the quiet three a.m. ceilings and my whole job was to find my way back to him. I spent a lot of years chasing that man. I never caught him.

And one day, sitting at the kitchen counter at oh-five hundred with a cup of coffee in my hand, it hit me. *He doesn't exist anymore.* That version of me isn't lost. He isn't hiding in some quiet corner of my life waiting for me to come reclaim him. He's gone. And maybe he's supposed to be. That thought felt heavy. Heavy the way a folded flag is heavy in your hands when it's not your child, but it might as well be. Heavy because admitting it meant accepting all of it, every mistake I made, every loss I carried, every moment I had spent rewriting in my head, trying to make it land somewhere softer. No edits, no rewrites, no "what ifs." Just acceptance.

Underneath the weight of acceptance, quietly, almost embarrassed to show itself, there was relief. I didn't have to fix the past anymore, didn't have to make it make sense, didn't have to turn it into something it wasn't. It had already done its job. It shaped me. Not into someone broken, but into someone awake.

I'm going to ask something of you in this book that nobody asked of me when I needed it most. I'm going to ask you to look at your story. Not the highlight reel. Not the version you tell at the bar when somebody asks if you ever saw combat. Not the one you tell your spouse. Not the one you tell yourself before you fall asleep, the one where the outcome was different. The whole story. The messy parts. The painful parts. The parts you swore you would never speak out loud.

I'm asking because I know what it costs to carry a story you refuse to look at. I've paid that bill. I've watched men I loved as brothers pay that price. I've sat across the table from spouses whose hands were shaking around their coffee cups, trying to figure out who the person across from them had become, while that person sat in a chair pretending they were fine.

I'm not asking you to look at your story so we can fix it. It can't be fixed. That's not how stories work. Inside it is the truth about who you are now, and you can't move toward who you're becoming until you can see and accept it. Somewhere inside yours, buried under everything you've been told it means, is the truth about who you are now. Until you can look at that, you can't move toward who you're becoming.

Let me tell you who I'm writing this for. I'm writing for the door-kicker who can't sleep without the television on. For the pilot who can't drive past a memorial without pulling the car over. For the medic who still sees that one face every time they close their eyes. For the cop whose hands started shaking three years after the call, and they can't figure out why. For the firefighter who told their crew "I'm good" so many times the words lost their meaning. For the dispatcher whose voice

When the uniform comes off,

the war doesn't.

was steady on the radio while their world quietly came apart in their headset. I'm writing for the veteran who walked into the kitchen this morning, smelled the coffee, and cried for reasons they couldn't name.

I'm also writing for the woman sitting next to him. The one who has watched him drift for years and doesn't know how to ask him to come back. The husband whose wife came home from the deployment, but only some of her did. The kids who learned to read the room before they learned to read books. The mother who worries every time the phone rings late. The father who never speaks of his son's third tour, because he doesn't know what to say. The silent half of every uniform. I see you, too. This book is yours.

Nobody wears trauma alone in a household. The veteran wakes up at three in the morning, and within a few months the spouse is waking up at three in the morning. The first responder stops talking, and the kids learn to whisper. The trauma may have been earned in one body. It gets paid for by everyone in the house.

So, when I write to the warrior, I'm writing to the family. When I write to the family, I'm writing to the warrior. You're one team quietly fighting two different versions of the same war. Here's a hard truth. When the uniform comes off, the war doesn't. When Life 2.0 begins, Life 1.0 does not get erased. We carry it home. Into the grocery store and the parent-teacher conference. Into the wedding receptions and the funerals. Into our marriages and our jobs and our friendships. Into the way we hold a fork and the way we sit with our backs to the wall. We carry it whether we know it or not, whether we admit it or not.

To the families, the silence isn't aimed at you. When the man you love comes home and goes quiet at the dinner table, when the woman you married won't talk about the deployment, the person inside still doesn't fully trust what would come out if they let it. They're protecting you from what they're still learning how to carry. The wound under the silence isn't aimed at you, even when it lands there anyway.

I'm not writing this from above the experience. I'm in it with you, just further along. Same road. Same weather. I've been walking it a little longer, and I've made enough wrong turns I can flag a few of them for you. The shift I'm describing, the day I stopped being a victim of my own life, didn't come from a book, or a therapist. It didn't come from a chaplain, and it didn't even come from my wife, though God knows she earned a medal for the years she stood in the doorway of my silence and led our family. It came from one realization. There is no going back. That version of me, the one who raised a right hand at eighteen with a head full of hope and a body that nothing had broken yet, isn't on the other side of this. He isn't the prize for getting better. He's gone. I'm still here. The question wasn't *how do I get back to him.* The question was *who do I become after my yesterdays?* Sit with that question for a minute. It looks small on the page. It's the most important question I've ever asked myself. The military doesn't teach it. The academy doesn't prepare you for it. It's the question waiting for you the moment the uniform comes off, the moment you hand in the badge, the moment the rotation ends. Most of us are so unprepared for it that we look around for somebody to give us the answer, the way somebody used to give us our orders.

Nobody is going to give you the answer. That's the bad news. The good news is you get to write it. *Who do I become after my yesterdays?* That single question changed the shape of my life. It changed how I saw my failures, how I saw the friends I lost, how I sat at my own kitchen table. How I shut others out. How I thought I was weathering this storm alone. Once I stopped trying to recover the man I used to be, I had room to meet the man I had actually become. Not the version with the medals on. Not the version in the official photo. The real one. Scarred. Slower to trust, faster to forgive. A little softer in the eyes than I expected. Quick to let tears flow from my heart and slow to wipe them from my cheeks. Carrying things I wished I didn't carry, but stronger in places I never knew strength could grow. That man wasn't broken. Every single thing that happened to him had made him into who he was, sometimes brutally and sometimes beautifully. Once I could look at him without flinching, I could look at my story without flinching.

Why am I telling you, in the very first chapter of this book, about the day I stopped telling my story from a place of pain? Because I want you to know I'm not writing to you from above. I'm working on the same things you are. I've been at it longer, and I've made a lot of mistakes you don't have to repeat.

A lot of us spend years trying to outrun our story. We try to drown it. We medicate it. We bury it under work, under achievement, under the next thing and the next thing and the next thing. It always catches us. Honestly, the greatest fear is the quiet and a pause. We tell ourselves, *if I can just keep moving, it can't catch me.*

What I learned, late and hard, is the story isn't your enemy. It's the only honest record of your experiences that made you who you are now. What you would have died for, what you almost did die for, who you were when no one was watching, who you became when everyone was, and what you live for. Your story didn't ruin you. It revealed you. When you can see that, really see it, a different kind of strength shows up. The kind that isn't ashamed of scars. The kind that's proud of them, because they made you who you are. We are the experiences of our yesterdays. The decisions and the indecisions, the actions and reactions and inactions of the days behind us, all of it made us who we are. Our tomorrows

Your story didn't ruin you.

It revealed you.

depend on how we take that experience and use it to write the next chapter.

I want to be careful here. I know what some of you are doing right now. You're reading this, nodding along, and quietly saying to yourself, *yeah, easy for him to say. He doesn't know what happened. He doesn't know the day I'm thinking about right now.* You're right. I don't.

I have sat with men who did things they will never tell their families, sat with women who came home from deployments carrying things no chaplain has a clean answer for and stood next to spouses who held it together for so long that when they finally cracked, it wasn't a tear; it was a flood. I have watched a nineteen-year-old paramedic try to explain why he can't go to his cousin's wedding, because his cousin's wedding is in the same church where he worked a code last year.

A veteran told me once, words I will carry the rest of my life, "I don't know how to tell my family I'm sinking in quicksand." Think about that for a second, *Quicksand.* Not drowning, not falling, not breaking. Sinking, slowly, with a grip you can't argue with. That's what so many of us are walking around in, behind our masks. Our jobs look fine. Our families look fine. The Christmas card looks fine. And underneath the surface, we are sinking by inches, and we don't know how to say it out loud because the past made you who you are. We are the experiences of our yesterdays.

The decisions and the indecisions, the actions and reactions and inactions of the days behind us, all of it made us who we are. Our tomorrows depend on how we take that experience and use it to write the next chapter.

Here's what's true about quicksand. The harder you fight it, the deeper you go. The more you flail, the tighter the grip. You cannot will your way out of quicksand, or push-up your way out, or run harder, or out-discipline your way out. There is only one way out of quicksand. Somebody else must reach in. And somebody else must be willing to reach. And you must be willing to take that hand. When someone offers their hand while they are also struggling it is no longer just help, it is love.

That's a hard sentence for a warrior to read. We were trained to be the ones who reach. We were trained to be the help, not to need it. The whole architecture of who we believed ourselves to be was built on being the person other people could count on. Admitting we're the one in the quicksand can feel like a kind of treason against our own identity. It isn't treason. It's honesty. And honesty is the first move every single one of us must make if we want to walk out of this thing standing.

That's part of what this book is. A way to start the conversation when you don't have anyone around to start it with. I'm not going to promise you that what's in these pages will fix you. No one can fix you, not because you're a lost cause but because nothing in you needs fixing. Something in

Nothing in you needs fixing.

Something in you needs translating.

you just needs translating. The pain speaks a language no one taught you how to hear. Your job, and mine alongside you, is to learn how to listen to it. Not so it can run your life but instead stop running your life from where you tried to lock it away. We're going to talk about the masks and what's underneath them. About identity, who you were inside the uniform, who you're still becoming outside of it. And about families, because no one wears trauma alone. And about what it takes to ask for help, and what it means to give it. There's also a difference between getting back to your feet and walking forward. Bouncing back is a beautiful thing. It will save your life. It saved mine. It isn't the whole story. We'll get to the rest of it when we're ready.

For now, just sit with this.

You don't have to fix your past tonight, forgive anyone tonight, or understand it. You don't have to make it make sense or turn it into a Hallmark card or a TED talk. You just need to stop running from it and stop pretending it isn't yours. Because it is yours. Every chapter. The proud ones and the shameful ones. The brave ones and the broken ones. The ones you'd put on a recruiting poster and the ones you wouldn't tell your closest friend. When you can stand in it without flinching or explaining, without apologizing or looking away, something quiet and powerful happens inside you. You stop needing the world to understand your journey. Because you do. That, my friend, is enough to start.

There's a phrase I want to leave you with at the end of this first chapter, the way you'd put a small thing in your pocket and carry it. No matter how far life takes you, no matter how many doors close, how many uniforms come off, how many funerals you attend, how many versions of yourself you must bury along the way, you can always *learn how to come home to yourself.* Not the old you and not the recruiting-poster you. The real you. The one with this book in your hands and a story that has been waiting a long time for someone to look at it without looking away.

I'm asking you to look. I'll be here when you do.

Let's begin.

CHAPTER 2

THE MOMENT YOU CAN'T UNSEE

Once you see it, you don't get to unsee it.
That's the moment everything turns.

I want to tell you about a moment you may not have words for yet. Most of us mark our lives by the event. The trauma that haunts our every moment. The one we locked in the emotional vault because we are just not ready, or able, to deal with it. It is the explosion, the crash, the bullet, the diagnosis, the phone call or the KIA notification at the door. The shift you came home from and couldn't stop staring at the ceiling. The morning the doctor walked out from behind the curtain with a face you understood before you heard the sentence.

You can probably name yours with the date, the time of day, what you were wearing, what the sky looked like. The break is sharp. Years later, when most of life has gone soft and blurry, the break is still crystal clear. Maybe yours was a vehicle on a road in a country whose name you barely say out loud anymore. Maybe yours was a hospital hallway. Maybe yours was a kitchen at midnight. Maybe yours was a uniform you took off for the last time and a closet you couldn't close after. Mine was 14 September at 1535 hours.

I knew before I knew that I knew. Wow, that is going to be a hard one to get past my editor, but it says it the only way that veterans know this feeling. First responders know it. Spouses know it from the other side of the door. The call you almost made, the message you almost sent, the action you almost changed because something in you wouldn't sit still. That sense something's about to happen. The prickle at the base of your skull, the hair lifting on your neck.

I woke up on September 14, 2003, with that feeling. It was a Sunday in Mountain Home, Idaho. I was a Thunderbird, callsign Elroy, on the back end of a long show season. Ten shows in a row, two more shows behind us in Reno and a short hop up to Idaho. Another show in front of us. Something was wrong with this one. Nothing was routine or normal. Before my feet hit the hotel floor, my gut was already telling me something I didn't want to hear.

I called my wife, Terri, in Las Vegas. The kids were fine. The house was fine. Nothing back home explained it. I told myself it was the travel, the rush, the fiftieth-anniversary year of the team. Busy times often feel heavier than average days. I slipped into my flight suit and went in early. In the briefing room, I sat down with our operations officer and tried to put it into words. "Something's just not right," I said. I asked to swap my opening maneuver, the Max Climb with Split-S, for my backup. A simple request and a simple change. Noone in the crowd would have felt the difference. He reminded me, in military style terms, I was a skilled aviator, chosen for my ability to fly the aircraft. Request denied. He wasn't wrong about my skill. He just couldn't see what my body could already feel. Anyone who has worn a uniform has had this conversation with a teammate, a leader, or with themselves. The voice that says don't go in there yet, don't take that call, something is off about today. Sometimes you get to listen to it. Sometimes you don't. I didn't. Twenty-Five Seconds, takeoff to impact. I replay it most every day in my mind.

We took off. I called "Six on the roll," surged the jet down the runway, lifted into a steep climb, rolled inverted, and pulled toward the top of the loop. Hundreds of times in training I had flown the same maneuver. My instruments said I was where I was supposed to be. My instructor's voice was in my head like a hymn, 'trust your numbers.'

As I apexed at the top, nose tracking down through the horizon, training said I was committed. Past a certain point in a maneuver like that, you cannot abort. You can only finish. Then the world told me the truth my numbers wouldn't, the ground was too close.

There was no panic. What I felt was a calm I had never met before, the kind that drops over you when there is genuinely no room left for fear. My body started executing emergency procedures my mind had not yet ordered. Engine, fine. Gear, up. Eject? Too low. Inverted. No survival. I pulled the nose away from the children and families watching. I rolled the jet so its trajectory would slip between the crowd and the tower, so the wreckage would land where no one was standing. I scanned the orange fence and saw individual faces, every spectator I will never know yet see them every day, looking up with anticipation not yet turned into horror.

Training does not make you brave. It gives your body a script when your mind is too far behind to write one. Every veteran and first responder who has done the job long enough has felt this. The drills you complained about, the reps you ran half-asleep, the hand-over-hand muscle memory. That is what shows up when everything else leaves the room.

What training cannot do is make the decision for you. I decided not to eject. The captain stays with his ship. I told myself that. I meant it. I started a maximum performance pull and committed to ride it in if I had to.

Then I thought of Terri.

Training does not make you brave. It gives your body a script when your mind is too far behind to write one.

I thought of her standing in our kitchen on Spotted Pony Drive, getting the call. I saw her drop to the floor. I saw our kids run in to ask what was wrong. I thought of every move we had made because of my career, every deployment she had endured as a single mother, every time she had said yes to my dream. I owe it to her to try to live.

The next thing I knew, the canopy was lifting away from the aircraft. I looked down. My left hand was grasping the ejection handle, holding it against my chest. My right hand was still flying the jet, exactly as I had instructed it to.

I now call them my fighter pilot hand and my family hand. My left hand made a decision my brain had voted against. Some people will read that as instinct. Some will read it as God. Some will read it as the wife I love refusing to let me leave. I have been all three of those readers, on different days. I am at peace not picking one. What I will say is this, the body keeps track of what we love. Long before we make the speech, long before we write the letter, long before we tell anyone. The body knows whose face it intends to come home to. Spouses of warriors, hear me. The work you do, the years you carried, is not invisible to us. It shows up in our hands at the worst moment of our lives. Your name is in our muscles.

The seat fired. Forty times the force of gravity in pure acceleration. Smoke rolled over my legs. The parachute snapped open. My world went black. The next thing I knew, I was standing on the ground.

The sky was clear. The sun was bright. I felt every joyful moment of my thirty-one years pour into me at once. Then I caught up to my own life and remembered where I was. Mountain Home. I ejected. There was no fire, no wreckage, no parachute. Something about shock, it is not what the movies show. Shock is the world arranging itself into a clean, plausible story your mind can handle. I looked down at my flight boots. There was not a speck of dirt on my red show suit. Well, this is it, I thought. I am dead. This is the afterlife. I cupped my face. My hands came back bloody red. I looked up. A parachute drifted down in front of me and collapsed. I was not dead. I was just finished believing the story my mind had given me. I waved across the field at our safety officer to let the team know I was alive. I started to walk toward him. On my third step, training kicked in again reminding me of the state of severe shock pilots are in after ejection. Recognize the symptoms. Do not move. I had lectured that warning in classrooms for years. Now I was inside the lesson. I backtracked the three steps to where my parachute dropped me down. I waited. Somewhere very near me, though I could not yet see it, my F-16 was burning. The flash fire of jet fuel had already passed over the patch of dirt where I had come down, and the survival kit tethered to my seat had hit the earth ahead of me, kicking up a circle of dust that smothered the flames where I would land.

The body keeps track of what we love.

If you have ever survived something you should not have survived, you know this feeling. People will tell you for the rest of your life it is not possible for you to be alive. And you will nod, and you will say I know, and a quiet part of you will go on living inside the impossibility, trying to make sense of the gift.

While I was lying in the dirt waiting for the fire chief, my commander was already on the radio. He knew our story would hit the news before any official notification could reach my home. He ordered another pilot to call my house. It is the call every military spouse rehearses without meaning to.

Terri was in our living room watching the movie Jumanji with the kids. The phone rang in the kitchen. She picked it up.

"Terri, it's Danno."

"Hi, Danno."

"Terri, there's been an accident."

"Danno, did Chris wreck his rental car on the way to the show?"

"No, Terri. There has been an aircraft accident, and we don't know if he is okay..."

She did not hear the rest. She dropped the phone and slid to the floor. As the wife of a fighter pilot, she was already certain what came next, a chaplain at the door.

Spouses, this part is for you. There is no preparation for that call. Drills are for us; the waiting is yours. We train, and

Traumatic Memory is loyal

to feeling, not to fact.

you wait. The arithmetic of military marriage is not equal, and we don't say that often enough.

In the emergency room at Mountain Home, I demanded a phone. The lines were jammed because of the crash. A young airman, maybe eighteen years old, picked up a landline and commanded an emergency break-through from the operator. He handed me the receiver. Terri answered, and through the line I could hear her heart bleeding out.

"Hey, babe. It's me. I just wanted you to know I'm okay."

She remembers that call differently than I do. I remember her yelling. The emotion of the day poured out in emotion. She remembers staying calm and happy to hear I was still breathing. We will agree to disagree. We were both there. We were both scared. The truth is that traumatic memory is loyal to feeling, not to fact, and after enough years you learn to make room for two true versions of the same minute. If you and someone you love remember a hard day differently, let it be. You are not lying to each other. You are protecting each other from inside two different bodies.

After a helicopter ride on a backboard to the trauma center in Boise, experts told me everything that could be wrong was...then about 10 hours later they unstrapped me and told me thirteen of my twenty-four vertebrae had dislocated. Three ribs dislocated. Legs bruised black from the parachute opening. Nothing broken. The doctor shook his head at impossibilities and said, 'you are going to walk out of my trauma center.'

A few days later, Terri flew out. We immediately embraced in what we still call the greatest hug ever known to mankind. I held her and tried to apologize, without words, for almost making her a widow. Then I pulled back, and we both knew something was off. I asked her to take me to the hospital. A flight surgeon's technician measured me against a wall, five feet, eight inches. For nine years, my medical record had listed me at five feet, ten and a half. The ejection had compressed my spine by two and a half inches. Over the next year, doctor after doctor told me that kind of compression was anatomically impossible. They repeatedly said there isn't enough cartilage in the human body to lose that much height permanently from a single ejection event without catastrophic vertebral fracture. Each time, I gave the same answer, 'I understand, Doc, but the fact remains I'm two and a half inches shorter and still standing.' I first realized it when I hugged the love of my life and she suddenly seemed taller than ever.

This is the part of trauma nobody warns you about, the things it changes that do not show up on the test. Your height. Your sleep. Your tolerance for crowds. The way your shoulders sit. The way you turn your whole body to look behind you because your neck won't anymore. The taste of your favorite food. The patience you used to have with your kids' noise. The way certain songs land. The way certain movies, Jumanji in our house, forever get turned off in the first thirty seconds without explanation.

Trauma is not only what happened. Trauma is what your body did with what happened, and goes on doing, in private, while you try to live.

If you are an EMT, a cop, a soldier, a nurse, a firefighter, a corrections officer, a dispatcher, a 911 operator, a chaplain, a flight crew member, a combat veteran or anyone whose work has asked your nervous system to do things human nervous systems were not built to do then listen carefully, you are allowed to have invisible injuries. You are allowed to grieve the person you used to be. The person who was two and a half inches taller. The person who slept through the night. The person who could go to the Fourth of July and not flinch at every explosion. You are allowed to grieve them, and you are allowed to keep going.

When Terri and I boarded the plane home from Idaho, we made a decision without ever having a conversation. We chose not to talk about it. We did not sit down and say let's not. We just didn't. Years went by. We grew our family through adoption. I served at the Pentagon, then Turkey, then Afghanistan. I commanded a squadron that won top fighter training squadron of the year. I made Colonel. And I did not sleep.

For most who experience a trauma, they ask themselves three questions. First, *why did it happen.* Then, *why did it happen now.* Finaly*, why did it happen to me.* My situation was different. After any aircraft mishap in the Air Force, a safety investigation then an accident investigation do their job of answering those. For me, the question which weighted down my everyday was, *why did I survive what experts say is unsurvivable.* For thirteen years, I carried this in silence. Regardless of which question is your anchor, it is equally heavy. The moment I want to focus on is the moment I broke.

Most nights before a flight, I lay awake. When I did sleep, I jolted up drenched in sweat and did not know why. Every time I put on a G-suit, terror rolled over me. The strange mercy was the moment I climbed the ladder into the cockpit; the fear and anxiety stayed on the ground. I told myself that meant it was under control. I told myself I would quit flying if it ever climbed up there with me. Translation, I told myself a story so I would not have to do anything about what I knew.

Veterans, hear this without flinching. Compartmentalizing is not the same thing as healing. We are very, very good at the first one. We were trained for it. It is a feature of the job... the ability to put a thing in a vault, lock the door and walk into the next mission. The vault is real. The vault works. The vault is also not where things go to be processed. The vault is where things go to wait.

For thirteen years, my vault waited. Then a friend and fellow Air Force officer finally called my bluff. He asked me to give a keynote to a group of business leaders about my crash. He convinced me to bring Terri. The event was scheduled a year out, a few months before my retirement, so I told myself I had time. Then I sat down to build the presentation.

I will not tell you it was hard. I will tell you it was like opening my chest with my own hands. Every photograph, every video clip, especially the cockpit audio, reopened it. I thought about this event every day for thirteen years, and yet somehow, I had never once embraced it. Sleeping got worse. I became irritable, jumpy, hot.

Since Terri was to attend the presentation with me, we sat in our living room and practiced. I cued the first video. Five seconds in, Terri said 'I can't' and ran out of the room. We both cried. The audio had taken her straight back to a phone call thirteen years before. That is how memory works. You can outrun it for a long time. You cannot outlast it. It is more patient than you are.

We kept practicing. Slowly, we got through the videos without breaking. Slowly, I got through my talk without my voice catching when I said her name. The night of the keynote, I genuinely thought I would pass out before going on. Now or never. I went on. We made it through. The audience cried. Terri and I cried later, in private, for different reasons than we had cried before.

I want anyone in uniform, or married to it, to understand what happened in those months of preparation. It was not that telling the story healed me. It was that telling the story forced me to meet the story, finally, with my whole body. What I had filed away as memory, my body had been carrying as injury. The injury wanted attention. It got it. If you have a story like this, and only you know if you do, there is no version of moving forward that does not eventually involve turning around and shaking hands with the thing you survived.

There was one more piece I had not told her. I had been diagnosed with PTSD. My doctor at Beale Air Force Base, Colonel (Doctor) Paul Gourley, who had become a friend, who knew me as well as anyone besides Terri had quietly walked me into a psychiatrist's office after I lost my temper in his clinic over a flight waiver. He sat through the verbal explosion. Then he sat with me on the other side of it. Wingman work, the medical version.

I had not told my wife. At every appointment, the psychiatrist asked me if I had told Terri. At every checkup, Paul asked. My answer was the same, 'I have not found the right time.'

I want you to notice something. I stayed with a doomed aircraft. I pulled an ejection handle outside the survivable envelope. I landed in a fireball I could not see and walked away. And the conversation I could not bring myself to have was a kitchen conversation with my best friend with whom I had grown up with since we were 12. That is not weakness. That is what stigma does inside a strong man.

On a simple, average Friday night, as we stood in our kitchen cooking dinner, it just came out. "Terri, there's something I need to tell you." She read my face. She gave me the look that has been there for thirty years. "Terri, I have PTSD." As you read earlier, there is no version of moving forward that does not eventually involve turning around and shaking hands with the thing you survived.

She said causally, 'I know. I sleep next to you. Did you think I didn't know why you wake up drenched in sweat? I didn't know we were hiding it. I just thought we didn't talk about it.'

Read that twice if you need to.

I had spent months convinced this revelation would devastate her. She had been living with the symptoms the whole time. The only person who did not know was me. Spouses, you already know. You already know more than we have told you. You know our breathing patterns, our triggers, the songs we skip, the dates we go quiet. We do not get to surprise you with our struggle. The only thing left to do is name it, together, out loud, so it isn't a private burden anymore.

After that night we started talking about everything. From my side, from hers. From the side of the kids who had been small when it happened, and the kids who had come into our family afterward. We retired. We moved back to Alabama, where we both started. We did not finish healing in that moment like I had hoped. The reality is we started healing. There is a difference.

If you have read this far, there is a reason. Maybe you ejected. Maybe you didn't, but something in your life ejected you anyway. A diagnosis. A deployment. A door you had to kick in. A trauma the official paperwork never accounted for. A long quiet drive home from a scene you could not unsee.

I am not going to give you the platitudes. We have all heard them. Time heals. Be grateful. It could have been worse. Those phrases are not wrong, exactly, but they are not enough, and we know it. Here is what I will say. The body knows before the mind does. Listen to it earlier than I did. If your gut is telling you the day is wrong, that is data. So is the sweat at three in the morning. So is the song you cannot listen to. So is the movie that must be turned off in the first thirty seconds. Your body is not malfunctioning. It is reporting. Training will save your life. Training will not heal your life. These are different jobs. Honor them both.

The ones who love us already know. The hiding is its own injury, and it adds up over years, and the people we are protecting are mostly protecting us back, in silence, on the other side of a kitchen. Survivor's guilt is real. Survivor's obligation is also real, and I prefer it. Guilt looks backward; obligation looks forward. Obligation says I am here when others are not and I owe somebody, myself, my family, those who didn't make it, a life lived on purpose.

The people who didn't come home would not want us to spend the rest of ours apologizing for breathing. They would want us to use it. That is the deal I made on a backboard in Boise, on a phone line to Las Vegas, in a kitchen in California, on a porch in Alabama where Terri and I drink our coffee while the sun comes up over a horizon I should not have lived to see on the tomorrow I almost lost. I made it to see another sunrise. If you are reading, you did too. This is the clarity with which I live my tomorrows. It is the one I challenge you to work toward. People talk about clarity like it's peaceful. The fog lifts and the world is in soft light, and you breathe in and feel grateful. Real clarity has edges. It is sharp. The past revealed you. The revelation is yours to use. Until you find clarity there is an exhaustion of carrying a narrative you have outgrown. I had been letting the past govern a future it had no business running. Remember, the story you keep telling about what happened is either building you or holding you. It cannot do both.

Let me tell you what the moment looks like, in real life, for real people I have walked beside. It doesn't arrive with thunder. It arrives somewhere ordinary. It arrives in a Lowe's parking lot, where a retired Marine sat for forty-five minutes with the engine off, because he heard himself about to tell his wife the same story for the thousandth time and, for the first time in his life, he felt the urge to tell the rest of the story. It arrives at three in the morning, on a couch, where a firefighter recognized she was about to send a text she had been sending every September for fifteen years, on the anniversary of the call that changed her, and her thumb hovered, and she set the phone down. It arrives in a deer stand, where a Vietnam veteran told me the conversation he had been having with himself in his own head for fifty years had finally gone quiet. In the quiet, he finally heard himself for the first time in a long, long time. It arrives mid-sentence, in conversation with somebody who doesn't know your whole story, when you hear yourself about to deliver the rehearsed thing, the explanation, the version you've used for a decade, and something in you stops it before it lands. It arrives in a folding chair at the back of a church, after a service for somebody who didn't make it, where a paramedic finally let himself say, silently, only to himself, that he had been carrying the same name in his pocket for eleven years, and it was time to either set it down or build a life around it on purpose. It arrives in a thousand quiet places, to a thousand quiet people, on no schedule and with no warning.

You stop because something in you recognizes the story you have been telling is over. *And what comes next is entirely up to you.* I want to tell you what changes after the moment, because the change is rarely what people expect. The pain doesn't vanish. The grief doesn't lift. The wound doesn't close because you finally looked at it square. What changes is smaller, and bigger, all at once. You stop running the tape. The mental loop, the rehearsed account, the running list of how you were wronged, it doesn't disappear, but it stops playing on its own. You can pick it up when somebody asks. You can put it down when nobody is asking. It stops running you. You stop arguing with the past, replaying the moment you wish you had handled differently, and trying to win an argument with somebody who isn't in the room and may not even be alive anymore. The argument finally ends because you set it down. You stop waiting. Most of us, after a break, are quietly waiting for something... an apology, an explanation, a reckoning, a miracle, a phone call, a return. A clean ending nobody is going to deliver. The moment of clarity is the moment you accept the apology isn't coming, the explanation isn't coming, the clean ending isn't coming, and you stop arranging your life around their arrival. And you suddenly have time. Time you didn't know you had. Time the past has been quietly stealing for years. *That time is yours now.*

I want to take a beat to speak to the families reading this. This moment is available to anyone in the house. There is the spouse who has been the pillar for twenty years and one morning over the kitchen sink realizes she has been holding a story about herself, 'the strong one,' 'the one who handles it,' 'the one who doesn't fall apart,' and the story has eaten the woman underneath it. There is the parent who has been mourning a son or a daughter for so long the mourning has become the whole shape of the day, and one afternoon, weeding a flower bed, hears something quiet inside say, he would not want me to live the rest of my life in this despair.

The story you keep telling

is either building you

or holding you.

It cannot do both.

There is the adult child who has been waiting, since they were nine years old, for the parent who came home from war to come the rest of the way home, and one day finally accepts that some part of that homecoming is theirs to make for themselves. Each of you has your own version of this moment. Your own past with a date on it. The same right to set down what is no longer yours to carry. Nobody in the house gets to grow forward while everyone else is still running the tape. This work, when it works, becomes a household event.

That is the gift buried inside the hardest thing you have lived through. I'm not going to feed you the lesson, or wisdom, or everything happens for a reason. I don't think it's what you need. I'm not even sure I believe most of those. What I do believe is this, the hardest thing you have been through was the most honest mirror you have ever stood in front of. It showed you yourself with no filters. No flattery. No comfortable story. No version you've practiced. No press release. Just you. And you are still here. *Which means you are still building.* Sit with the word *building* for a second. Building is putting one good thing on top of another good thing, day after day, until something stands. You don't need a blueprint of the original house. You need a piece of ground. You may have lost the original house. A lot of us have. The ground is still here. The ground is enough to start.

I want to leave you with something before we close this chapter. The chapters ahead will ask you to use what the mirror showed you. We will use it to make better decisions from here. That is what clarity is for. *Clarity is a tool.*

Some people treat clarity like a verdict. They mistake awareness for accusation. They take what the mirror showed them and use it as evidence in a private trial they keep losing on purpose. We are going to do this differently. We will use clarity to decide what to keep and what to set down. What to invest in and what to walk away from. What to say yes to. What to say no to. Who has earned a seat at our table and who has been sitting there on borrowed time. The chapters ahead start small. We name what is in front of us. We hold it. We set it down. Tomorrow, we pick it up again. And the day after. This is how a life gets rebuilt. One honest look at a time.

Take a breath. The next chapter will be here when you're ready.

CHAPTER 3

THE SILENT HALF OF THE UNIFORM

She never raised her right hand. She surrendered her career, raised four children, carried a mortgage, and moved their home 18 times in 23 years, all in defense of this nation.

In the last chapter, Terri said, "I sleep next to you. Did you think I didn't know?" That sentence broke me. It also kept me. And it was true. She had been living with what I had been hiding for thirteen years. The diagnosis was mine. The years were ours. This chapter is for the ones who already know. The spouses. The parents. The children. The caregivers. The friends. The people who watched us drift, who held the family together while we were gone, who memorized our breathing and our triggers and the songs we skip without ever being told to. The ones who choose a seat first in the restaurant so they can face the wall and let us see the crowd. You are the silent half of the uniform. Most veterans keep a photograph somewhere, in a wallet, taped inside a footlocker or pinned above a workbench in the garage. The photograph is of the people who waited. This chapter is for them.

We talk a lot in this country about the men and women who serve. We salute them at ballgames. We thank them at airport gates. We pin yellow ribbons to old oak trees and place decals for the back of the truck. We should. They earned every word of it. Behind every set of dog tags is a kitchen table where someone else sat alone for a year. Behind every deployment patch is a child who learned to ride a bike without a father there to catch the fall. Behind every honorable discharge is a spouse who became a nurse, a mechanic, a counselor, a roofer, a tax preparer, and a single parent, all between Tuesday and Thursday, because that is what the calendar required.

They are the silent half of the uniform. It is past time we said so out loud. Long before there was a Department of Defense, there was a porch light left on. Long before there was a benefits office, there was a woman at a window. The

American military family is the oldest unit in our armed forces, and the only one never formally mustered.

When the orders come, the family receives them. They just don't get to read them first. A spouse learns the cadence of "thirty days," "six months," "one more rotation." A child learns to count the calendar in pages instead of weeks. A parent learns to sleep through the call that does not come, and to wake instantly to the call that might. The whole family learns to live in two time zones at once, the one on the wall, and the one where their soldier is.

While the soldier is gone, the house keeps running. The dog still gets sick. The water heater still breaks on the coldest night of the year. The school still calls about the report card. The car still skids on a patch of black ice. The bills arrive in their plain white envelopes, indifferent to where the other signature is. None of it pauses. None of it waits for the homecoming.

Keeping the home fires burning is real work. It is repairing the screen door, sitting up at three in the morning with a feverish toddler, and explaining to a seven-year-old, again, why Daddy missed the recital. It is making Christmas happen on a Tuesday in February because that is when he gets back.

They were enlisted by love. Civilian life rarely names this loneliness. It is the loneliness of presence at a distance. The other parent is alive. The other parent loves the children desperately. The other parent will, God willing, be home. For now, the other parent is a voice on a video call that freezes at the worst moments, a name signed at the bottom of a letter, a folded flag of a body still very much breathing on the far side of the world. So one parent does the work of two, a single-parent in a two-parent picture.

They become the reader of bedtime stories and the disciplinarian, the cheerleader and the budget-keeper. The one who bandages the knee and the one who explains, with steady eyes, why Mommy or Daddy is not at the parent-teacher conference. They learn to answer the unanswerable question, "When is she coming home?", with a tenderness that does not crack, even when their own heart is.

They sit through PTA meetings where other couples sit together, solo in church pews where other families sit together, through the long, ordinary Saturdays married people take for granted. They smile when neighbors say, "I don't know how you do it." They smile because the truth is too long for the grocery aisle. The truth is they do it because there is no one else who will. The truth is they do it because the children are watching. The truth is they do it because love, in a military family, is a verb conjugated in the future tense.

Terri did this for years while I was at the Pentagon, in Iraq, in Turkey, in Afghanistan, on the road with the Thunderbirds, then the road with another command, then just on the road again. She raised our children. She moved our house. She held the line. She sat through the school events alone. She counted the calendar in pages. She lived in two time zones, the one in our kitchen and the one wherever I was.

I did not see most of what she did. The work doesn't get seen. It gets done. There is a Saturday in 2005 I think about often. I was deployed. Terri was at our house in Alabama with our kids. The air conditioner broke, the dog decided to play 'can't catch me' in the subdivision, our oldest rode the bench again at his baseball game because the local coach says his father has never been to a game so Terri must be a single mom, still have not understood that logic, then I called. Her tone shifted automatically to positive regardless of the weight on her shoulders. Terri reassured me everything was fine, nothing to worry about at home so just take care of myself.

Recently, as we were preparing to lead a veteran marriage retreat, Terri revealed what she had been taught so many years before. As the young spouse of a new fighter pilot, the commander's wife gave a 'deployment' talk to prepare them for what deployment life was like. One of the key facts stressed in the meeting...

> *Everything is fine, even when it isn't. The squadron is deployed and in combat. They need to be hyper-focused. Make sure you never tell them the problems you are dealing with back home. You are strong. You can handle it, that is your job.*

Veterans talk about compartmentalization often; it was not until this point I realized compartmentalization impacted our families as well. Multiply that lecture by every spouse, every weekend, for the entire post-9/11 era, and you start to understand the size of what we're talking about.

One day the door opens. The duffle bag drops in the hallway. The deployment ends. A new, quieter deployment begins. Nobody briefs you on this one. The person who comes home is not always the person who left. Sometimes the changes are small, a flinch at fireworks, a preference for the chair facing the door, a habit of scanning rooftops on a sunny afternoon. Sometimes the changes are larger, nightmares that arrive uninvited, a temper with a shorter fuse, long silences where there used to be laughter. Sometimes the changes are invisible to everyone except the one person who has memorized this human being. The one who knows what 'normal' looked like, and notices, before anyone else, when it does not. That person becomes a protector. A softer kind of protector. A fiercer kind, too. They learn which holidays are hard and why. They learn the difference between a quiet evening and a dangerous one. They learn how to clear a room of triggers before he walks in, how to pivot a conversation away from a memory she has not told the children about, how to sit beside the bed and breathe in a steady rhythm until his does the same.

They become advocates. They sit in VA waiting rooms with thick folders and thicker patience. They learn the acronyms, TBI, PTSD, MST, VSO, C&P. They make the phone calls their veteran cannot bring himself to make. They translate "I'm fine" into the language of action. They argue with insurance companies, schedule appointments, refill prescriptions, read benefit letters out loud, and write the appeals when those letters are wrong.

They guard the door of a house the war sometimes still tries to enter. They do it without rank, without ribbon, without recognition. The payment is the quiet conviction the person they love is worth the fight.

Terri became a protector somewhere in the years between 2003 and 2016. I cannot tell you the exact date because she never made it official. She just took up the post. She watched the calendar. She knew September 14th was approaching before the rest of the world did, every year, and made sure something gentle was on the schedule for that day. She knew which Air Force gatherings would be hard and quietly arranged for me to be on the road for a few of them. She knew the songs and the smells and the pressure changes I couldn't name.

There are statistics for almost everything in the military from re-enlistment rates, casualty figures, dollars spent to sorties flown. There are far fewer numbers for the cost the family pays. There is no medal for the spouse whose career was rerouted six times by PCS orders. There is no citation for the teenager who attended four high schools in four years and learned, somewhere along the way, that lasting friendships are a luxury other kids take for granted. There is no plaque for the grandmother who raised the grandchildren during the second tour. There is no Purple Heart for the wife whose marriage survived three deployments and one diagnosis, or for the husband who learned to live with a wife who came home and did not, for a long while, come back.

The price of service is shared. It has always been shared. The bill arrives at different addresses. In our house, the bill arrived as thirteen years of silence. Terri carried that. She carried my diagnosis before I told her about it. She carried my sweat-drenched nights without ever asking why. She carried the Jumanji rule, the cockpit-audio rule, the days the calendar reminded her without explaining anything. She carried the man I had become because I had not figured out how to come home all the way. She carried me.

The check I wrote on the steps of the recruiter's office had her signature on it too. I just didn't know that for a long time. Most of us don't.

If this book is honest, it cannot end on the doorstep where the soldier walks back in. The story continues into every kitchen and every car ride and every long, ordinary evening of the years that follow.

We owe the military family more than thanks. We owe attention. We owe childcare that understands a 0400 alert. We owe schools that know what a deployment cycle does to a fifth grader. We owe employers who do not penalize a spouse for a résumé with gaps shaped exactly like their country's wars. We owe mental-health care for the partner as well as the patient. We owe communities that learn the names of the people who waited, and not only the ones who returned. At minimum, we owe them the courtesy of being seen.

They are the silent half of the uniform. They have been there the whole time. This chapter, and the gratitude inside it, belongs to them.

Please thank the silent half of your uniform. This chapter is in honor of the spouses, parents, children, and caregivers who served without ever putting on the uniform.

CHAPTER 4

SURVIVOR'S OBLIGATION

I am still living tomorrows I almost lost.

My favorite mornings I sit on a porch in Alabama and watch a sunrise I almost did not live to see. I bring Terri coffee. The dogs settle on the boards. The first light comes up over the trees on the east side of the property. We don't say much. We don't have to. Both of us know what the morning is. It carries an obligation. I want to spend this chapter telling you what I mean by that.

There are two kinds of strength people develop after hard things. The first is resilience. Resilience is the ability to *bounce back*. It is the muscle letting you take a hit, get back on your feet, and keep moving. It is how you finish the deployment. How you make it to the funeral. How you keep going to work the day after the call. Resilience saves lives. It saved mine.

Resilience has a ceiling. It aims to return you to where you were before the hit. Back to the version of you who existed before the ambush, before the diagnosis, before the door. As we said in chapter one, that version is gone. The trip has no destination.

The second is what I'd like you to spend most of this chapter sitting with: post-traumatic growth. It is the ability to bounce forward — to take what happened to you, walk through it, and let it shape you into a version of yourself who didn't exist before. Resilience says, I can survive this. Post-traumatic growth says, I can become someone because of this. Both are real, and both matter. Most veterans I know have lived inside resilience for years and never once been told the second strength existed.

Before we go any further, a few ground rules. You don't have to share anything you don't want to. Growth does not mean being over it. Growth and pain can sit in the same room, and most of the time they do. This chapter is not about fixing trauma. It is about noticing growth and learning how to protect it.

Two psychologists put a name to it in the mid-1990s. Lawrence Calhoun and Richard Tedeschi, working at the

Resilience says, I can survive this.

Post-traumatic growth says,

I can become someone because of this.

University of North Carolina at Charlotte, spent years sitting with people who had been through the worst things human beings can be put through. They kept noticing the same thing. After enough time, in some people, real change started showing up because of how those people walked through what happened. They studied it carefully. They called it post-traumatic growth. In the years since, the research has expanded into veteran populations specifically and the answer is the same one Calhoun and Tedeschi found in the first place. Growth is real. Growth can be supported. Growth is not given, it is grown.

Three words get used as if they mean the same thing, and they don't. Recovery is getting back to function. Resilience is bouncing back from a hit. Post-traumatic growth is bouncing forward into something you would not have been without the hit. You can be recovering, resilient, and growing all in the same week and most of you are, whether you noticed or not. None of the three is better than the others. They are different jobs the mind and the marriage are doing at the same time.

Five changes show up most often. I'll give them to you in plain English, and I'll give each one to you twice, once in the voice of the veteran, once in the voice of the spouse because in a veteran marriage, growth is rarely a solo act.

1. Small things matter more.

Coffee on a porch becomes the answer to a question you didn't know you were asking. The sunrise stops being scenery and becomes motivation. A spouse's hand in yours has weight. Time becomes specific, and you stop spending it the way you used to.

The veteran: I notice the quiet now. I notice my kids breathing in the next room.

The spouse: I stopped sweating the small stuff after the deployment. I know what big stuff looks like.

2. You're stronger than you thought.

You catch yourself doing things you would have said you couldn't do. You walk into rooms you used to avoid. You hold conversations you used to dodge. You realize you have been underestimating yourself for a long time — by training, by habit, by humility, by a story somebody else told about you.

The veteran: I can handle hard things now. I have already done the hardest thing.

The spouse: I held this family together for fifteen months. I am not the person I was before that deployment.

3. Relationships go deeper.

Your contact list gets shorter. The people who matter come into sharper focus. The conversations you have go further than the ones you used to have. The small talk gets harder. The real talk gets easier.

The veteran: I don't waste time on shallow friendships anymore. The brothers and sisters I have, I would bleed for.

The spouse: My friendships are deeper now. I know who showed up.

4. New paths open.

You walk a few of them. Some of them you would have laughed at five years ago. A pilot starts a foundation. A medic becomes a chaplain. A spouse goes back to school. A retired cop who could not sit still begins peer-support work and discovers he is better at this job than the one he left.

The veteran: I never thought I'd go back to school. I never thought I'd lead a peer-support group.

The spouse: I became a nurse because of what we walked through. I never would have chosen that field on my own.

5. Big questions move.

Faith, or the lack of it. Meaning, or the search for it. The framework you used to live inside doesn't fit the same way anymore. You build something more honest.

The veteran: I know what I am here for now. I didn't before.

The spouse: My faith is harder and more honest now. I ask better questions.

These five domains mark post-traumatic growth in plain language. The research has more to say. Before we go further, four things I want both of us to hold; four things that keep growth honest.

First. Growth lives next to the wound, never in place of it. Post-traumatic growth and post-traumatic stress can coexist. You can carry the diagnosis and still build something useful on the ground beside it. You can wake up at three in the morning soaked in sweat and still pour coffee for somebody who needs you at six. This goes for moral injury too, the wound that comes from acts of commission, omission, or witnessing, which is its own kind of weight and which often goes unspoken. Growth does not require that any of it be resolved first.

Second. Growth lives next to treatment, never in place of it. If you have a therapist, keep going. If you take medication, keep taking it. If you have a chaplain, a sponsor, a peer-support group, hold onto them. Growth is what happens over time, on top of the work, not instead of it.

Third. Growth is chosen, second by second, minute by minute, hour by hour, by the person doing it. The trauma did not give it to you. The choices you made afterward did. Two people can go through identical events and come out very differently. The difference is what they did with it. An analogy I have carried through my life to remind me of this is the story of a set of twins. They had an abusive alcoholic father. One twin grew up to achieve more than anyone imagined possible. The other lives in the same town, clouded by his own alcoholic haze. When the first is asked why he turned out the way he did, the answer is always, because of my dad. When the second is asked why he turned out the way he did, the answer is always, because of my dad. One chose to use the lessons of growing up in an alcoholic house as the flint to launch his rocket to different stars. The other saw a hopeless future of repeating his family's alcoholic legacy and used it as an excuse. We may not control the events of life. We always control our response.

Fourth. Growth is something you build. The pain was not the lesson. The pain was the wreckage. The growth is what you put up on the ground next to the wreckage, one good piece at a time. Hold those four. They will keep this chapter honest, and they will keep you honest with yourself when somebody hands you a quote about silver linings.

Here is the thing the textbooks took a long time to figure out. Post-traumatic growth doesn't only happen inside a person. It happens between people. Researchers studying military families found that spouses of veterans don't just absorb the cost of the trauma and there is a cost, which I'll get to in a moment. They also experience their own growth. The research calls it vicarious post-traumatic growth. Their faith changes. Their priorities change. Their sense of what they can survive changes. Some of the most profound growth in a veteran marriage happens in the spouse, and it tends to go unnamed because everyone in the room is looking at the one who deployed. So let me name it. If you are the spouse of a veteran, what you have carried is not nothing. The research has a name for it. Secondary traumatic stress is real. Caregiver burden is real. In some studies, the rates of post-traumatic stress symptoms in partners of veterans approach the rates in the veterans themselves. You are not making it up, and you are not weak for feeling it. And the same long struggle that has cost you something has also, for many of you, grown something. Both of those sentences are true at the same time.

Your spouse didn't cause your trauma, but they can become the safest place your growth lives. Growth in a marriage is not a solo performance. It is a duet. Trauma puts pressure on a marriage. Most couples can name the pressure points without being told. One partner pulls away, the other chases, and both feel rejected. Emotional numbing gets read as disinterest. Hyper-independence, *I don't need anyone, becomes I won't let you in.* The body stays in mission mode at home, and irritability becomes the background hum of the house. Protection gets misheard as rejection. Sleep goes sideways. Physical distance becomes emotional distance. None of that is a sign your marriage is broken. It is a sign your marriage has been carrying something heavy.

Growth shows up in a marriage too, and the same couple will usually have both lists running at once. Conversations get more honest because the surface ones no longer satisfy. Boundaries get clearer , both partners get better at saying yes and no to the right things. Time together becomes intentional rather than incidental. Values come into alignment because you have already figured out what matters. A shared *we survived* identity takes shape, a story only the two of you have. And compassion gets bigger, for each other, and often for other people who are hurting. If you look honestly at your marriage, you will find yourselves in some of column one and some of column two. That is not contradiction. That is what real growth in a real marriage looks like.

A fair question at this point is, how. How does a person, or a couple, move from surviving to building. The research has been clear, and what it says lines up with what veterans and their spouses tell me when they have been through it. Growth is not a switch you flip. It is a set of habits you choose, again and again, until they become the shape of your days. None of what follows is required. All of it helps.

Give it time. Post-traumatic growth is rarely something you notice in the first six months, and it cannot be rushed. It shows up most clearly in hindsight, usually months and years after the worst of it. If you cannot see it yet, that is not failure. That is the timeline.

Let yourself feel the whole range. Growth comes from struggling with the trauma, not from clamping down on it. Grief, anger, fear, numbness... they are all part of the work. Suppressing them does not move you forward. Acknowledging them does.

Find people who can hold the weight. Strong, safe relationships are one of the strongest predictors of growth in the research. Tell your story to people who will listen without trying to fix it. If saying it out loud is too hard, start with writing it down. Voice notes count. A letter that never gets mailed counts.

Make meaning. Growth shows up when you start asking the bigger questions. Not why did this happen, that question rarely has an answer, but how has this changed me, and what matters more now. Notice the shift in your values, the people you keep close, the things you no longer have patience for. That noticing is the work.

Put it on paper. Journaling, writing, art, storytelling, they all help the mind integrate what the body has been carrying. Even a few minutes a day for a week, written honestly, can move something loose. Name the strengths you did not know you had. Most people underestimate what they survived and what it took to survive it. Look at what you got through and look at how. Emotional, practical, relational, list the skills you used and the ones you grew. They are evidence. Connect to something larger than yourself. For some people that is faith. For others it is community, creativity, the outdoors, service to someone else who is hurting. Growth tends to take root when life gets bigger than the wound.

Protect one small thing together. If you are doing this as a couple, pick one. Not a list. Not a five-year plan. One thing you are going to protect this week either the Tuesday walk, the phone down at dinner, saying thank you out loud when your spouse listens to you, or praying together once. Small commitments that get kept are how marriages grow. The growth that has already begun in you is fragile in some places and tough in others. What grew in us deserves protection, not pressure.

Survivor's remorse, or survivor's guilt, the academic language is accurate. I prefer my own. Survivor's obligation.

Survivor's obligation is the calling to make the tomorrows you almost lost intentional. To take what happened and use it the way you would use any hard-earned piece of information about how the world works. I prefer obligation to guilt because they go in different directions. Guilt asks, why did I survive. Obligation asks, what will I do with the survival. Guilt looks backward. Obligation looks forward. Both are real. Most of us who survive things spend time inside guilt. Some of us live there for years. Guilt, by itself, is not a place to live. Obligation is a way to use what guilt taught you.

I want to take a beat for the couples reading this together. Growth doesn't happen only inside a person. It happens between people. Trauma puts pressure on a marriage in specific, recognizable ways. One partner withdraws while the other pursues. Emotional numbing replaces the connection that used to be there. The wounded partner becomes hyper-independent and reads any offer of help as a threat to their own sense of self. The other partner reads the protective distance as rejection, when the distance is the only way the wounded one knows to keep them safe.

If any of those sound familiar in your house, you are not broken. You are responding the way human nervous systems respond when one of them has been through more than it was built for. Growth shows up in marriages in specific ways too. Honesty gets deeper. Boundaries get clearer. The time you spend together gets more intentional. The values you live by start lining up. The two of you develop what therapists call

Guilt asks,
why did I survive.

Obligation asks,
what will I do with the survival.

Guilt looks backward.

Obligation looks forward.

a shared 'we survived' identity, the sense that whatever you face from here, you have already faced harder, and you faced it together. Here is the line I want both of you to carry out of this chapter. Your spouse didn't cause your trauma. They can become the safest place your growth lives.

That sentence is for the warrior reading this and the spouse reading it next to them. It is also for the warrior reading it alone, who has been holding the trauma without showing it for years. The growth has been quietly building anyway. Letting your spouse or another veteran see it is part of the work. Let me show you what this looks like outside the research.

There is a Navy corpsman who carried a name in her pocket for nine years. She runs a peer-support program now. She walked through the wound. She named it. She let it teach her. She sits across kitchen tables from younger corpsmen and tells them they are not alone.

There is a fighter pilot I flew with who lost his wingman. He came home and led young aviators for twenty years. He leads them with a softness in his voice he didn't have at thirty. He says the softness came directly from the loss. The leadership downstream of it is different.

There is a wife of a retired Marine who almost left. She didn't. She mentors other military spouses through the years she almost didn't survive. She tells me she would have nothing useful to say to those women if she had not been so close to the edge herself.

None of those people are healed in any movie sense. All of them are still in it. All of them have chosen, again and again, to use what happened to them as material. That is the survivor's obligation. I made my own deal on this journey to survivor's obligation in pieces, on different days, in different rooms.

The first piece was on a backboard in Boise. After ten hours strapped to a backboard hearing that I probably would never walk again and they were not sure if I would make it, the trauma surgeon shook his head over me and told me I was going to walk out of his trauma center. Lying there with my body in pieces but somehow whole, I knew, without having language for it yet, I was going to owe somebody something for the rest of my life.

The second piece was on a phone line to Las Vegas. When I heard Terri's voice on the other end and realized she had been told her husband was dead before she was told he was alive, I knew the obligation had a name. The name was hers. I owed her the years she had almost lost.

The third piece was in our kitchen in California. The night I told her about the diagnosis, when she said "I sleep next to you. Did you think I didn't know?", the obligation got bigger. I owed our marriage the conversation I had been postponing for thirteen years.

The fourth piece is the porch in Alabama. Out there with the coffee, with the sunrise, with the wife who refused to leave the doorway of my silence, the obligation became permanent. It became the shape of how I get out of bed.

Your deal will be yours, in the rooms where it finds you. I am telling you the deal is real, and there is a moment in your life when you will know you are standing inside one, and you will have a choice. *Take the deal.*

The chapters ahead don't have the answers. The answers aren't mine. They're yours. I have the questions. I have the discipline to sit with you while you find your own answers. I have the willingness to share my answers when they help. That is what survivor's obligation looks like for me.

What grew in us deserves protection, not pressure.

CHAPTER 5

WHAT WILL YOU LIVE FOR?

Each day has 86,400 seconds.
There are no carryovers, no redos.

As the sun appears over the tree line, I drink my coffee on a porch in Alabama. Most days a computer sits on the small table next to me. Some days I write in it. Some days I just look at it. Either way, the day in front of me does not start until I have asked myself one question. *If today were my last day on this earth, would I do what I am about to do?*

The question came from a chapter I wrote in an earlier book about intentional living. After 2003, after the kitchen, after Alabama, I realized the question I had written for the general reader was the question that would define the rest of my own life. For someone who almost lost a tomorrow, the question is not theoretical. It is accounting.

In *Aiming Higher, A Journey Through Military Aviation Leadership*, I asked the reader a hypothetical. Tomorrow, somebody hands you $86,400 in cash. The rule, spend it by midnight or forfeit the rest. How carefully would you spend each dollar? Each day has 86,400 seconds. Same rule. No redos and no carryovers. What we find is most of us are more careful with our pennies than with our seconds. For survivors of hard things, the math gets sharper. You are aware, more than most people, of how few seconds anybody is guaranteed.

Survivor's obligation is intentional use of the seconds you almost didn't get. The next question is, intentional toward what?

Before you read further, I challenge you to define success in your life in three to five words. Say it out loud if you can. Write it down. This is not an easy task. Some people I have worked with took up to two years to do this simple exercise. The goal is a single phrase small enough to fit in your head, and broad enough to apply across every domain of your life, career, marriage, parenthood, faith, all of it. It is the spine of how you spend the seconds. Most people freeze the first time they try this. They have spent forty years working toward something they cannot define in three to five words. Do it anyway. The first version is not your final answer. The first version is your starting point. For trauma survivors, the answer often shifts after the break. The definition you carried at twenty does not survive what happens at thirty or forty. The new definition is more honest, because it is built on the ground you live on now. It is also at this point, many realize how shallow their definition of success was as a pay raise, a promotion or an award. While these may be important steppingstones on the journey of life, they are not true success. As the years stack up your experience, what most realize is life is more about living your why than achieving a shallow definition of success.

A simple two questions to find your why. First. At the end of the longest, hardest, dirtiest day of work you have ever had, when you are driving home tired enough to fall asleep at the wheel, what brings a smile to your face? What makes you say, in your head, I can't wait to do that again tomorrow? Second, on the day you take your last breath, what answer do you want to be holding for the question, 'why did I live this life?' Sit with both. Write them down if you can. Your WHY lives where the two answers overlap.

If you still need more details on how to develop this, look to Ikigai. In Japanese culture, it roughly translates to "a reason for being" or "a reason to get out of bed in the morning." It's the quiet sense of purpose that gives ordinary days their weight, the thread that ties effort to meaning.

The concept is often illustrated as the overlap of four circles: what you love, what you're good at, what the world needs, and what you can be paid for. Where all four meet, you find your ikigai. Passion lives at the intersection of love and skill. Mission emerges where love meets the world's needs. Profession sits between skill and pay and vocation forms where what the world needs aligns with what it will pay for. Ikigai is the center where every circle touches.

What makes ikigai practical, rather than just poetic, is that it asks you to take all four dimensions seriously. A pursuit you love but can't sustain financially becomes a hobby. A skill the world rewards but you don't care for becomes a grind. The goal isn't to chase any single circle but to keep moving toward the place where they converge. Treat ikigai less as a destination to arrive at and more as a compass: a way of checking whether the life you're building is one you want to wake up for.

For survivors, those questions become a contract, they become your survivor's obligation. A trauma forces the long-day question and the deathbed question into the same room as your morning coffee. You cannot ignore them. My answer to both is the same. What I want to do tomorrow, and what I want to be holding when I die, is a record of having used the tomorrows I almost lost, living each to the fullest. That is my WHY. It is also my obligation. Yours will be different in shape and the same in spirit, if you are honest with the questions.

Once you know your WHY, the next move is your WHAT. The specific accomplishments that make the WHY real. Stand in front of a whiteboard. A piece of paper works. A phone screen works. The structure is what matters. Draw a line on the right. This is the finish line. To detail this, flash forward to the end of your life. As you look back and pop the champagne to celebrate, what are you celebrating? This forms the details for your finish line. Next draw a line on the left side. This is your today. Detail every aspect of situation, resources and attitude. Define where you are in this moment.

In the space between these marks, list the accomplishments and milestones that must happen for your WHY to be made real. Each one is a must-have. Have a hard talk with yourself about what really matters and why each item earns the space on the board. Under each item, write the reason it is a must-have, and what is lost if you don't get there. The reason underneath each item is what carries you when motivation runs out.

Now sequence backward. Start at the right side, the finish line, and work back toward today. What needs to be true the year before you die? The decade before? Five years from now? One year from now? This month? This week? Start with the end in mind. Combat-proven senior officers work this way. Olympic medalists work this way. My favorite example of this is the moonshot. On May 25, 1961, John F. Kennedy stood before Congress and committed the United States to landing a man on the Moon and returning him safely to Earth before the decade was out. The country had no rocket capable of the trip, no spacecraft capable of the landing, no navigation capable of the precision, and no plan for what would happen after the boots touched the surface. NASA had eight years and seven months to figure out everything. The first major thing they did was pick three landing site options. Before the engines, before the suits, before the math, they decided where on the moon the boot was going to come down. The destination came first. They built everything else backward from it.

Any survivor focused on post-traumatic growth will tell you they are on the road. The road has a destination. They are walking toward it on purpose. Today is the combined total of every yesterday. It is also the starting point for every tomorrow. The work of survivor's obligation is making sure those two truths line up.

Now that you have your WHY as your obligation, the next move is to name what the obligation is made of. To find this, answer three questions, in order.

First, name what survival cost you. What are the bills you are still paying, detail the years you lost, recognize the people who waited and look at the body that bears the scars.

Then, name what survival gave you. This one is harder. Veterans flinch from claiming it. Survival gave you perspective, the capacity to recognize your own kind across a parking lot, a list of what you will not tolerate, the kind of knowledge you cannot gain from a book. None of it makes the cost worthwhile but all of it is yours to use.

Finally, name who you owe... yourself, your spouse, your kids, your team, the people who waited, the ones who didn't make it, and the younger version of yourself who got you here. Name names. Specific names. Abstract obligation evaporates by lunchtime. Specific obligation stays.

I close every day with a checklist then the same question I learned to ask after I almost lost my tomorrows.

Checklist Step 1: Today was a success, yes or no & why.

Checklist Step 2: Today, I learned...

Checklist Step 3: Today, I improved...

Checklist Step 4: Today, I struggled with...

Checklist step 5: My focus for tomorrow is...

Then the final question: If I knew this was my last day, would I live it the same way? If the I , I sleep. If the answer is no, plan for a better tomorrow. Tomorrow is allowed to be different. The question is a debrief in the sense the Thunderbirds and SEAL teams use the word. Every show. Every mission. Review, learn, adjust, fly again.

Your life deserves the discipline of a Thunderbird debrief. *Live intentionally.*

The next chapter is another question. We will keep asking them together, in order. Tonight, ask the debrief question and answer it honestly. Tomorrow, ask the morning question, *If today were my last day, how would I live it?*

That is the work.

CHAPTER 6

SOMEDAY IS A DISEASE

Two text messages rocked me in the same week. The first came from a group I've worked with for years. We call it the Military Mentorship Mastermind. A small circle of people who push each other to do work that matters. We were planning the next project. One of us proposed a delay of a few years. The reply was a photograph. A graveyard. White stones in straight rows. Underneath the picture, a quote.

> *"The graveyard is the richest place on earth, because it is here that you will find all the hopes and dreams never fulfilled, the books never written, the songs never sung, the inventions never shared, the cures never discovered, all because someone was too afraid to take that first step, keep with the problem, or determined to carry out their dream."* Les Brown

The text sat in my pocket for the rest of the afternoon. I knew the line. I had quoted it from stages. I had not, in any way I could honestly defend, been living it.

The second text came the next morning from Terri. We had spent the weekend on the porch talking about retirement. Smiles across our faces as we planned dreams, travel, time without the calendar interrupting us. We had even put a rough timeline on a few items. The conversation ended, as several before it had ended, with one of my Sunday-night specials, '*Someday we will.*' She didn't argue with me. She didn't even bring it up the next morning over coffee. She just sent a text. A picture of nature. And one line.

> *Someday is a disease that will take your dreams to the grave with you.*

I read it once, then sat with it. Then I read it again. Then I put the phone down and looked at the porch the way you look at the room of a friend after a hard truth has been told. I have spent years on stages telling audiences to live intentionally. I had been living it less than I claimed. The two texts arrived in the same week the way two warning lights come on at the same time. The system was telling me something. I needed to listen. This chapter is a framework to move forward after you listen.

My mother had a potholder in our kitchen growing up. Round, fabric, burned in a few places from years of use. On one side it said, in plain block letters, "Round TUIT."

I did not understand it as a kid. The other side explained it.

> *This is a Round TUIT. Guard it with your life. They are hard to come by. Most people delay their accomplishments with the same simple statement, "I will do it when I get a round to it." Now you have one. Now there is no excuse. (Paraphrased from memory)*

She kept that potholder in plain view for years. I think she was raising a son who needed to see it every time he opened the oven.

In our house, Terri and I have a different name for the same trap. We call it the Tuesday effect. The reference is J. Wellington Wimpy, Popeye's well-dressed friend from the 1930s comic strip, who borrowed money for hamburgers with the line, "I'll gladly pay you Tuesday for a hamburger today." He received the burger today and the bill was always due on a day that kept moving. Tuesday never came. Most of us have a Tuesday. The day we will get around to it, deal with our demons and write the next chapter of our lives. The day we will call the friend. The day we will take our spouse on the trip we have been promising for ten years.

For survivors of hard things, the Tuesday effect is more dangerous, not less. The time you postponed is the time you already almost didn't get. Survivor's obligation is what you do with the seconds you almost lost. Postponing them is the one move you cannot afford. Will Durant, paraphrasing Aristotle in The Story of Philosophy, gave us the line:

> *"We are what we repeatedly do. Excellence, then, is not an act but a habit."*

Survivor's obligation lives or dies on the truth in that sentence. The obligation is not a single decision you make on a backboard, on a phone line, in a kitchen, on a porch. The obligation is what you do with the calendar tomorrow. And the day after. Today. That means the work has to have a structure. The rest of this chapter offers you the structure. A close friend who leads in the asphalt industry, Bo Walters, taught me the following GSD process which changed my life in a positive way. I am thankful to have him in my life and for the fact he said to include this without concern about credit with this simple phrase, "use it in any way that has a positive impact on other's lives."

What season are you in? Before you build the structure, name the season. Different seasons of life ask different things of us. The framework is the same. The contents change. A few examples to help you locate yourself:

> Teen years: Finding your place. Building strengths. Recognizing weaknesses.

College or trade years: Moving from dependent to sponsor, student to worker, single to married. Figuring out the shape of an adult.

First decade of career: Establishing yourself. Starting a family if you choose one. Becoming the version of yourself the next decade will need.

Second decade of career: Riding the credentials you built. Deciding what next. Launching kids into their own seasons.

The years before retirement: Expanding outside work. Developing the give-back.

Retirement: Wrapping up unfinished business. Building legacy. Sitting with the question of impact.

Pick your season honestly. The one you live in, not the one you would prefer or the one you have already left. The season is the soil. Everything else grows out of it. Once you have your season, list the five things that matter most inside it. Call these the Most Important Things, the MITs. Five. Not seven. Not three. Five is small enough to fit on an index card and large enough to cover the territory of a season. Specific names. Concrete categories. Not values. Not virtues. The actual people, missions, and commitments you will give your best energy to.

My five, in this season, look something like this:

1. Terri: Our marriage as the safest place my growth lives, and the place where I owe the largest part of the

obligation. A focus of time, effort and emotion on her now, even though it will never make up for the times she was a single-parent in a two-parent photo. For the time she lived inside the window of my death before she lived inside the correction.

2. Our kids and grandkids: The legacy in motion. The people I missed twenty-three birthdays of who get my best now.

3. Alabama Veteran: The mission outside our four walls. The way the obligation extends to the men and women I never served with but recognize anyway. The obligation to my brothers and sisters to help them transition into Life 2.0 with a saddle and bridle on their demons.

4. This work: The book in your hands. The keynotes. The sit-downs at the back of banquet halls. The translation of survival into something useful for somebody else.

5. Faith: The work I do early in the morning before anybody else is up, the work I will not skip on a hard week. How I live under the guidance of 1 Peter 4:10, I paraphrase as 'use whatever gifts you have received, time talent and treasure, to serve others, as faithful stewards of God's grace in its various forms.'

Yours will be different. Five things, named on purpose, in the order they get your best energy.

Each MIT needs a cadence with details of the tasks to accomplish daily, weekly, monthly, yearly. Without a cadence, the MIT becomes a poster on the wall. For each one, ask the same four questions. What does growth in this look like daily? Weekly? Monthly? Yearly? If your MIT is your marriage, daily might be a real conversation, no phones. Weekly might be a meal alone together or a glass of wine on the porch as the sun sets on another beautiful day. Monthly might be a date that takes you out of the house. Yearly might be a trip with no agenda. If your MIT is faith, daily might be the morning devotional. Weekly might be a service. Monthly might be a service to somebody else. Yearly might be a retreat. If your MIT is your work, daily might be the discipline of starting before the email starts. Weekly might be a review. Monthly might be a project advance. Yearly might be a single major outcome. Specific. Named. Measurable. The four cadences keep the MIT alive between the moments you would otherwise notice it.

Inside every season, a few things must happen before you leave it. Those are the things to do Before I'm Gone From This Season, BIGs. Different from the finish-line list in the last chapter. That list is the whole life. The BIGs list is this chapter of the life. If you are in the second decade of career, BIGs might be something along the lines of launch the kids well, pay off the mortgage, write the book, build the program, take the trip, repair the relationship. If you are in retirement, BIGs might be see the grandkids in their hometowns, build the legacy gift, finish the project, write the letters. Limit yourself to a handful. Three to five. These are the items that, if undone when the season ends, will sit in the chest as the unfinished business survivors' obligation refuses to leave behind.

Non-negotiables are the bare minimum that keep your MITs alive. Daily non-negotiables are the things you do every day, no exception, regardless of weather, mood, schedule, or whether anybody is watching. Weekly non-negotiables are the rhythms that protect each MIT from drift. Monthly non-negotiables are the check-ins, the meetings, the deeper review. Yearly non-negotiables are the reviews, the trips, the retreats, the milestones. If a non-negotiable starts getting negotiated, the MIT it protects is in trouble. That is the early warning. Treat it as one.

If it is not on the calendar, it does not exist. Calendar every non-negotiable. Daily, weekly, monthly, yearly. The calendar is where intentional living is enforced. The calendar is where Tuesday becomes a real day instead of an excuse. Schedule your BIGs. Two per year, minimum one. Block the time. Defend it the way you would defend a flight you're briefed to be at. Energy follows MITs in order. The first MIT gets your first hours of the day, before the world starts pulling. The fifth MIT gets the time it needs, in its place, on its day. *Consistency compounds.*

That sentence is doing more work than it looks like it's doing. Every reasonable thing you do for an MIT, every day, on a cadence, compounds. Every reasonable thing you skip compounds the other direction. The math runs in both directions whether you watch it or not.

In chapter five, we ended on a debrief question, if today were my last day, would I have done what I did today? In this chapter, I want to add five short questions to the debrief. Five names for what intentional living produces in a life.

Today, who did I thank?

Today, who did I acknowledge?

Today, who did I appreciate?

Today, who did I impact?

Today, who did I inspire?

Five short answers, written in a notebook by the bed if that helps. The MITs and the calendar give you the structure. These five questions tell you if the structure is doing the work it was meant to do. Life is about living in community, in both moments and your days. What defines a life is not found in gestures alone, but in the quiet sum of our thoughts, our words, and our deeds, both is what we have done and in what we have left undone.

Excellence is a habit. Survivor's obligation is the habit of using the seconds you almost lost.

Tuesday is today.

CHAPTER 7

BUILDING A WINGMAN CULTURE

My life is in your hands, yours is in mine.

Wingman work in the medical version. That is what Colonel (Doctor) Paul Gourley did the day he walked me down the hall of his clinic to a psychiatrist. Paul was my doctor at Beale Air Force Base. He had been adjusting my back for a while. He had become a friend. The day my temper broke in his clinic over a flight waiver, he sat through the explosion. Then he sat with me on the other side of it. He saw what I couldn't see, a man who needed the next door opened, and he opened it. He didn't fix me. The job of a wingman is not to fix anyone. The job is to see what the other one can't see and act on it. That phrase, *wingman work*, has roots.

There is another piece of the story with Doctor Gourley I want to tell. The day I lost my temper in his office is the day he kicked the lock off my trauma vault. I first wrote about that experience in *Survivor's Obligation: Navigating an Intentional Life*. Paul and his wife, Melissa, were the first to read the book after Terri. When I asked their opinion, there was only one criticism. Paul said I had told the story wrong. He said the waiver he gave me that day was for the black T-38 in the fleet at our base, not the combat F-16 that almost took my life. I disagreed. What unleashed my trauma and anger was the thought of returning to the plane that almost took my life. We agreed to disagree. And disagree we did. Often.

One Saturday night around the firepit in Alabama, we were sitting with our wives on a tomorrow I almost lost. As we drank our first, or fifth, glass of scotch, Paul popped off about me not telling the story correctly. I popped back that I was tired of him lying about it and I was willing to take a polygraph to prove it. He agreed. At this moment, our loving wives, almost in unison, instructed us to sit down, shut up, sober up, and talk about it tomorrow. We did. At breakfast, we decided to settle this once and for all.

Two months later, we both met in Washington, D.C. to sit for separate polygraph exams. Finally, I could prove him wrong once and for all. The result, "Both passed their polygraphs with different versions of the truth."

The polygraph machine was not in the office on the day of the discussion. It did not know what was really said. What a polygraph measures is whether the person is telling their truth. In this case, each version was different. The truth is what you believe to be true. In communication, what matters is what the other person hears. As I said in Chapter Two, traumatic memory is loyal to feeling, not to fact, and after enough years you learn to make room for two true versions of the same minute. If you and someone you love remember a hard day differently, let it be. You are not lying to each other. You are protecting each other from inside two different bodies.

In flight, a wingman is the second pilot in a two-ship element. They fly on the leader's wing, see what the leader can't see, call the threats coming from the leader's blind spot, and stay in formation through the maneuver. The leader knows the wingman is back there. The wingman knows the leader is depending on it. Air Force Handbook 36-2618 makes the role official. It directs every Airman to know and understand it.

> *Airmen take care of fellow Airmen. A good wingman shares a bond with other Airmen. Air Force Handbook 36-2618*

The Airman's Creed names it before it names anything else. "I am an American Airman. Wingman. Leader. Warrior." Wingman comes first because everything else follows from it. Air Force Ace Francis "Gabby" Gabreski put it this way,

The wingman is absolutely indispensable. I look after the wingman. The wingman looks after me. It's another set of eyes protecting you. That's the defensive part. Offensively, it gives you a lot more firepower. We work together. We fight together. Wars are not won by individuals. They're won by teams.

Gabby Gabreski

In a cockpit, the working code is one sentence: My life is in your hands and yours is in mine. In every other room a survivor walks through after the uniform comes off, the sentence still has weight.

In the Air Force, the wingman role is structural. You don't have to construct it. It is there when you arrive, when you walk into the squadron, when the engine starts. The day the uniform comes off, the structural wingman disappears. Most retired veterans I know didn't see this coming. We assumed the network would carry. Some of it does. Most of it doesn't. The squadron moves on. The crew chief retires three years after you do. The unit deactivates. The men and women you used to call when the world went sideways are still your friends. They are no longer assigned to your six. After retirement, if you want a wingman, you build one.

The same is true for first responders. The shift schedule that put six other people in the same room with you for twenty years is over. The dispatch that knew your voice is somebody else's voice now. The brotherhood is real, and the structure is gone. What used to be automatic is now your responsibility to construct.

The role of a wingman comes from the basic fighting element of a fighter aircraft. The role has three duties. The same three duties translate cleanly into the work after the uniform.

First. Be prepared for any task. Always. The wingman shows up briefed, ready, and capable of stepping into the leader's role if the leader is taken out. In recovery, this means when your wingman calls, you are reachable. When your wingman is in trouble, you are ready. The day they need you, "I'm busy" is not a sentence in your vocabulary.

Second. See what the leader doesn't see. Do what the leader can't do. The wingman's vantage point is slightly different. They see the threat at five o'clock and the gear that didn't come down. In recovery, they see the drinking that crept up, the withdrawal from family, the story being repeated for the thousandth time. The mood that has lasted three weeks. They name what they see. The leader trusts they will.

Third. Do what the leader needs done before being asked. The wingman who waits for orders in combat arrives late. The wingman in recovery who waits to be asked, for the call, for the visit, for the sit-down, arrives after the funeral. Anticipate.

Together, the three duties produce one outcome. The wingman has the leader's six. The leader has the wingman's six. There is no third party required to make the system work. The principle that holds wingman work together has a name, Accountable interdependence. We hold ourselves accountable. We hold each other accountable. This happens not as a rule somebody enforces but as a practice the team agrees to. There are three pieces.

First piece. Each person holds themself accountable for their own performance. In recovery, I do my own work. I sit with my own story. I keep my own calendar. I do not outsource my growth to my wingman.

Second piece. Each person holds themself accountable for enabling the other. In recovery, when my wingman is doing the work, I make the conditions easier. I show up to support what they're building. I refuse to become the obstacle they have to manage on top of everything else.

Third piece. Each person holds the other accountable. This is the hardest one. It means I tell my wingman the truth even when the truth is uncomfortable. It means I name the drift when I see it. Love does not become a license to look the other way. If one of us fails, we all do. Thomas Reid wrote in 1785 about a chain whose strength is the strength of its weakest link.

> *"The strength of the chain is determined by that of the weakest links; for if they give way, the whole falls to pieces, and the weight, supported by it, falls to the ground." Thomas Reid, The Intellectual Powers of Man, 1785*

A wingman culture is a chain. For survivors, the implication is harder than it looks. The strength of your recovery community is the strength of its weakest member, on its weakest day. Which means the person closest to the ground deserves the most attention. Most communities build around the strongest. The wingman culture builds around the weakest link, every time. The weakest link is the one carrying the weight today and everybody else helps.

A wingman culture rests on a foundation of strong relationships, clear communication, active listening. Psychological safety sits on top of all of it. Psychological safety means I can tell my wingman the truth without it being used against me. I can say 'I'm sinking' without being told to suck it up. I can name the diagnosis without it leaking. I can describe the night I nearly didn't make it without becoming a project. A culture that punishes honesty produces performance, not truth. Performance is what got most of us this far. The work ahead requires truth.

The kitchen conversation between Terri and me, the one where she said "I sleep next to you. Did you think I didn't know?" only worked because the kitchen was safe. We had built that over thirty years. Some of you are starting from less. Start where you are. Build slowly. Trust earns at its own rate.

Being and having a wingman is a privilege. It is earned daily. The role grows with wisdom, knowledge, and transparency. Each action, inaction, and interaction either builds the trust or erodes it. The day you cancel a call at the last minute because you don't feel like having the conversation, you have erased weeks of deposit. The day you name the drift you've been seeing in your wingman, even though it costs you a hard conversation, you have made a deposit no one else could have made. The greatest value of a wingman is the vantage point. They see what you do not. You see what they do not. The angle is the gift.

Two questions to close this chapter, and to carry forward into the rest of the book.

Who has your six? Whose six do you bear?

Name them. Specifically. Specific names of specific human beings whose phone numbers you know by heart and who know yours. If you cannot answer either question, this week's move is to start. Send a text. Make a call. Pick up the phone with one specific person and say a sentence you have not said before. "I want to be your wingman in this season of life. Will you be mine?" Most of the time, the answer is yes. Most of the time, the other person has been waiting for somebody to ask.

My life is in your hands and yours is in mine.

Now go answer the call.

CHAPTER 8

THE MASK YOU PAINT

It takes strength to carry the invisible. It takes heart to keep moving forward when your soul is still catching up.

The battlefield is behind us. The medals are on, the flag is folded, and a lot of us are still wearing something else, a mask. Not the kind that protects from dust or disease but one forged from experience. A mask shaped by sacrifice, loss, and survival. Not made of fabric or armor, but of silence and strength. A mask that carries the weight of war without ever speaking its name.

The mask covers what we feel in private. It's the smile that hides the nightmares, the laugh that covers the guilt, and the strength that conceals the struggle. We wear it to protect the people we love from our pain, to keep our families from worrying, and to keep people from misunderstanding us, judging us, or pitying us. None of those we can stand. The mask is courage. It's the courage that doesn't show on a fitness test. It's the courage that holds a family together through a year of deployment, gets up the morning after the funeral, and walks into the briefing room when every part of your psyche wants to walk out. The outside of the mask, the one everyone sees, is the one you intentionally created to hide the parts you don't want others to see. The inside is the way you see yourself. The mask is not weakness. It is proof of courage. It takes strength to carry the invisible. It takes heart to keep moving forward when your soul is still catching up.

The mask is for the mission. A patrol. A briefing. A funeral where you can't afford to come apart in front of the family. A hospital corridor where the nurse asks how you're doing and you answer with the only word the job ever taught you for that question, *fine*. The mask is also for the years. It's for the question nobody trains you for, the question that arrives sometimes within hours of the uniform coming off and sometimes years later but arrives for almost every one of us. *Who am I without this?*

I became an Airman at eighteen. For twenty-seven years, the entirety of my adult life, that was the only world I knew, the only language I spoke fluently, the only way I knew how to introduce myself in a room. As I started preparing to retire, a strange terror set in. That isn't a word I use lightly. I ejected from an F-16 outside the survivable envelope of the seat. I stood next to flag-draped caskets. I flew combat. I led young aviators into rooms they came back out of changed forever. The thing that scared me most was the day I would have to take off the uniform and walk into a grocery store as a civilian. Because I didn't know how to be one.

The military is incredible at taking ordinary people and turning them into warriors. Teenagers off the street, through basic training, into a uniform, into a unit, into a mission, into an identity. The whole system runs that one direction. What the military is not good at is the other direction. They taught us how to be warriors. They didn't teach us how to be civilians again after the journey. Our retirement or separation felt like the military threw us out of an airplane without a parachute. To cope, we put on the mask. The mask is the last piece of the uniform, and it's the only thing we know how to wear when nothing else fits.

Almost two hundred thousand of us return to civilian life every year. Some thrive. Some find a new mission immediately. Some find a community of veterans who help them get reoriented. Most don't. Three out of four veterans report difficulty adjusting to civilian life after taking the uniform off. That's your neighbor, the man at the gas station, the woman in the next pew, the dad you saw at the youth baseball game last week, sitting on the third-base side, smiling, doing his absolute best. Behind every one of those statistics is a face, and on most of those faces is a mask that hides what they feel from what they allow to be seen.

The mask has two sides. A mask is a translation. On the outside is the calm, collected, put together face you present to the outside world. On the inside is the consolidation of experiences, traumas, triggers and everything you want to protect the world from and not deal with. The struggle happens on the gap in between.

The mask costs you. It costs your patience with the people who deserve your patience most, and the joy you would otherwise feel at small things. It costs you the ability to receive a compliment without rolling your eyes. It costs you intimacy and the language for what's inside you. And every year you wear it the mask gets a little harder to take off. It costs your family the version of you they remember.

The mask served a purpose. It still does, in its proper place. The harder question is what to do when the mask has outlived its proper place. What worked for me, and what I've watched work for hundreds of others, is putting the mask down a little at a time, in the right rooms, with the right people, until the face underneath remembers how to be the face. There's no schedule. There's no prescription. No two faces come out from under a mask the same way. Healing happens when your inside mask matches your outside one.

It started for me with one room. A doctor at Beale Air Force Base. A friend who walked me into a psychiatrist's office on a day I had lost my temper over a flight waiver. He sat through the verbal explosion, then he sat with me on the other side of it. Nobody made me take the mask off in that office. Nobody could have made me. What that office did was let me practice, for an hour at a time, in a room where the consequences of showing my internal mask, the one I truly saw myself through was acceptable.

Then the second room was a kitchen. A Friday night. Terri. *I have PTSD.* You read that conversation already. What I didn't say in that chapter is the mask didn't come off in one motion. It came off slowly, in the months and years that followed, conversation by conversation, with the woman who already knew.

Then it was a community. I finally trusted a few veterans with words I'd never said out loud, *I am struggling.* Then a few more. Eventually, it became a mission, a community of veterans and families who trust each other enough to let their walls down and heal together. A family of veterans doing exactly what this chapter is about, helping the next person take the mask off in a place where it's safe. That's the pattern, a safe room, a safe person, and a reason to take it off. You don't need all three at once or in any order, and they don't have to be perfect. Start with one and trust the others will come.

You don't have to keep wearing it. I know it feels like loyalty. It feels like honor. It feels like the kind of strength you learned in your first uniform. The people you served with would understand the mask, and they might be wearing one too. You aren't broken. The world that needed the mask, the world that called for it, the world that handed it to us and told us wearing it was the job you are not in it anymore. The world you're walking around in, the kitchen, the church pew, the Tuesday afternoon, the grocery store, doesn't require the mask. It requires you.

When you put the mask down, the face underneath is the one your family came home for, the one your spouse fell in love with, the one your kids needed to learn to read, the one the friends who didn't come home would recognize. Take it off in safe rooms. Put it back on if you must. Then take it off again the next chance you get. That's how this works. As you begin to let those around you see inside the mask, it will become easier. Easier for the inside of the mask, the way you see yourself, to get just a few steps closer to the one you put on to project yourself to the outside world.

A mask is for a moment. Your face is for the rest of your life. It takes whatever is happening inside you, the grief, the fear, the rage, the tenderness, the doubt, and translates it into something the world can handle. The mask says, I will give you a version of me that doesn't ask you to carry too much. I will give you a version of me that fits in this room, on this team, in this house. Most masks start out kind. The veteran wears one at Thanksgiving so his uncle's questions about "what was it really like" don't ruin the meal for everyone. The first responder wears one at her daughter's school play because she just came off a pediatric call and refuses to let that night follow her into this auditorium. The spouse wears one at the PTA meeting because she is too proud to let the other parents see what it has cost her to hold this family together for the past eight months.

Those are honorable masks. The cost of an honorable mask, worn too long, is the same as the cost of a dishonest one. *You are not dealing with the person underneath.* The most exhausted people I have ever met are the ones who told the truth too rarely. The truth is heavy. When you don't put it down, it doesn't disappear. It goes inside. It sets up shop in your shoulders, your jaw, your sleep. It shows up in the way you snap at your kids over nothing, in the third drink you didn't plan on, in the silence at the breakfast table your spouse has stopped trying to fill. The mask hides where you put the truth. The truth is still there.

A note for the families reading this, because nobody says it to you often enough. The mask is not aimed at you. It looks like it is. It feels like it is. When the man you love comes home and goes silent at the dinner table, it can feel like a door slamming in your face. When the woman you married won't talk about the deployment, it can feel like she's shutting you out of the most important part of her life. The mask is up because the person inside doesn't yet trust what would come out if they let it. They're protecting you from what they're still learning how to carry. That doesn't make it hurt less. The wound under the silence isn't aimed at you. It's aimed at a war you weren't in but are now living next to.

By the time you reached this chapter, you have done a lot of work. You have looked at your story. You have looked at the moment after the break. You have understood what the people around you have been carrying alongside you. You have a framework. You have a why. You have an operating system. You have a wingman.

Let's take time to examine your mask. Find a piece of paper. Draw a simple oval. Treat it like a mask. The mask has two sides.

The outside is what you show the world. It is the face people see when they ask, "how are you?" at the gas station and you say, "doing great, you?" without thinking. It is the face on your LinkedIn photo, your retirement portrait, your Christmas card. It is the version of you that walks into a room and decides what people are allowed to know.

The inside is what only you see. The face in the mirror at four in the morning. The face you wear when you're driving alone, and your favorite song comes on, and you're surprised by how much it gets to you. The face you wore the last time you cried, even if it has been a long time. The version of you nobody else has been allowed to meet.

Paint both sides.

The medium does not matter. Paint works. A pen on a napkin in a diner works. A page in your notebook works. The honesty is what matters.

For the outside, the face you show the world, sit with these. You don't have to answer all of them. Let the ones that catch your eye catch your eye and follow them.

What three words do you want people to use when they describe you?

What expression do you wear when you walk into a room you don't fully trust?

What do you want your spouse, your kids, your team to believe about you?

What would you never want anyone to think you are?

What part of your image have you worked hardest to protect?

When was the last time someone complimented you on something not actually true about you, and you let it stand?

For the inside, the face only you see, sit with these. Take them slow. You don't have to share them. You only have to look at them yourself.

When you are alone, what do you most often think about?

What are you most afraid people would find out?

What do you grieve and have never said out loud?

What part of yourself do you secretly admire and would never tell anyone?

What part of yourself do you secretly judge and have never confessed?

If you could let one person inside the mask, who would it be, and what would you tell them first?

This is wingman work. After you have done the exercise alone, take one item from the inside to your wingman. One item. Not all of it. Say it out loud, in a room with no audience, with permission to set it down and walk away when you're done. The kitchen between Terri and me, "I sleep next to you. Did you think I didn't know?", was a version of this exercise. She had already seen what was inside. I just hadn't said it out loud. When I finally did, the mask started coming off. One corner at a time.

That is how real growth happens, one corner at a time. You start by letting one trusted person see one true thing. Then another. Then another. You will keep wearing some kind of face in the world. The barista at Starbucks doesn't need your full deployment biography to make your latte. The mask, in some form, stays. What changes is this. The face you wear stops being a fortress. It becomes a door you can choose to open with the people who have earned the right to see what's behind it. You stop being a stranger to yourself. You can sit alone at four in the morning and recognize the person in the chair. You can walk past a mirror and not look away. You can stand in your own life without performing it. The goal is eventually to paint the mask and realize what you see on the inside is also what people see on the outside.

You cannot grow through a mask. Start with one corner.

CHAPTER 9

WHEN IT GETS HARD

We did not finish healing. We started healing.

There was a year I will not romanticize. It was 2016. I had agreed to give a keynote about the crash. A friend had asked. I had said yes. The event was a few months out, and I told myself I had time. Then I sat down to build the presentation. I will not tell you it was hard. I will tell you it was like opening my chest with my own hands. Every photograph reopened it. Every video clip, especially the cockpit audio, took me back to a kitchen on Spotted Pony Drive where Terri took a phone call thirteen years before. Sleeping got worse. I became irritable, jumpy, hot. I would wake up in the dark soaked through with sweat, not knowing why.

I had thought, going in, I was ready. That could not be further from reality. Veterans were trained to read setback as failure. The mission slipped and setbacks were corrected, fast and direct. The work of recovery does not run on a curve. The work runs on something more like a tide. Some days the tide is in. Some days the tide is out and the floor is mud. The same beach. The same body. Different conditions. The work continues regardless.

A setback shows up because the work is real. Real work moves the body. The body responds. Setbacks have specific shape after trauma. The mask wants back on, because the familiar face is the easier face. The body remembers how to wear it. The vault wants to close. The thing you finally named wants to go back unnamed. The wingman gets hard to call. The voice in your head says you have used your allowance. They have their own life. Don't bother them with this again. The calendar collapses. The non-negotiables you set become negotiable, in the order they were hardest to keep. The why questions feel hollow. The same questions that landed five chapters ago sound like words now. Just words. If any of those sound familiar in a hard week, you are inside the work. The work is doing what work does.

Some days the tide is in.

Some days the tide is out and the floor is mud.

Don't rebuild from scratch. The instinct in a hard week is to look at the whole structure. The MITs, the non-negotiables, the wingman, the framework, the calendar, the book in your hands. All of it. In a hard week, that is enough to freeze you. So, you do nothing. That is the wrong move. Pick the closest piece. The biggest can wait. One action at a time. That is how you do the work.

In 2016, the closest piece was the morning hour. I could not face the keynote prep. I could not call my wingman. I could not get through the cockpit audio without coming apart. The closest piece was the porch, the coffee, and ten minutes of silence before Terri came out.

That was enough to start the day.

The day after, the closest piece was the same. The day after that, the same. Three weeks of just the morning hour. Four weeks before I could call my wingman. Five weeks before I could sit through the cockpit audio without leaving the room. Five weeks looked like a long time when I was inside it. Looking back, it was the right pace. The pace was set by the closest piece, not by my schedule and not by my pride.

The body keeps track of what we love. I have said that earlier in the book. In setback, the body is also keeping track of what we are pushing too hard. A setback often shows up in the body before the mind names it. Sleep changes, appetite shifts. The shoulder you forgot about starts hurting. The drink you used to put down at one becomes two. The drive home from work feels longer. Read the body. The body has been carrying this longer than the mind. When you read a setback signal in the body, the answer is usually less discipline, not more. Sleep. Eat. Walk. Sit on the porch. The body is asking for the closest piece. Give it the closest piece.

If your wingman is the one in a hard week, your job is to stay, show up, make the call, sit on the porch, bring the coffee. Don't disappear. Setback in the wingman you are accountable to is the moment your accountable interdependence gets tested. Stay close. Hold the questions for the next good week, when the question can land without breaking the person. The hard week is for presence, not accountability.

If your wingman is the survivor, learn the difference between a hard day and a dangerous one. The hard day asks for company. The dangerous one needs resources. Know the numbers before you need them. The Veterans Crisis Line is 988 and press 1. Know it the way you know your own birthday. Know it before you need it. Know it for somebody else as much as for yourself.

I want to leave you with a sentence I learned in the year of the keynote. *We did not finish healing, we started.* There is a difference. The work is a road. Some sections are paved. Some are mud. All of them are the road. The road keeps going as long as you keep walking it. In a hard week, the only thing that matters is to keep walking. Pick the closest piece. Reach it. Then the next one.

That is the work.

Pick up the closest piece.

CHAPTER 10

TOMORROWS I ALMOST LOST

I should have died. That sentence opened this book. I want to close it from a different room. I am writing this on an early Sunday morning in Alabama. The sun is up over the trees on the east side of the property. Terri is in the kitchen. The dogs are on the boards. A coffee cup sits in front of me with the steam still rising off it. The morning is ordinary in every way the morning of 14 September 2003 was not. I want to walk you through what is here.

There is the kitchen behind me. This kitchen is not the kitchen on Spotted Pony Drive where Terri took the call. That kitchen is in a house we no longer own. The Spotted Pony Drive kitchen is where I almost made her a widow. This one is where I make her coffee.

There are the men and women who come up to me at the back of banquet halls after I walk off stage and say, very quietly, "I am not OK." There have been more of them than I expected.

There is a charity in Alabama whose board is filled with people I love. Alabama Veteran. Outdoor adventures. Peer mentorship. Leadership training. Suicide prevention. The men and women we serve are some of the men and women I would not have met if Boise had gone differently. There is the keynote story I almost stopped giving in 2016. I did not stop. The men and women who hear it are why.

There is the airman in the emergency room at Mountain Home, the one who got me a phone line when the lines were jammed because of the crash. He was eighteen, maybe nineteen. He commanded an emergency break-through from the operator and handed me the receiver so I could tell Terri I was alive. I never got his name. Wherever he is, he is in the count of what survival built. He is the reason Terri heard my voice instead of a chaplain at the door. There is this book. There is the unfinished version of myself I get to keep working on, on a porch in Alabama, in the seconds I almost did not get.

I want to say something to you directly before we close. Your tomorrows belong to you, and your obligation is yours to define. Your version of this work will look like you. That is the point. Somebody, somewhere, is hoping you make it through this season. Somebody is hoping you become the version of yourself who shows up. Somebody is hoping the years you almost lost get used. That somebody might be your spouse, your kids, your friend, your wingman. It might be a chaplain you met once. It might be the person you were at twelve, who would be proud of you for making it this far. It might also be somebody you have not met yet.

If you have read this far, you have done the work. You have looked at the story. You have named what you owe. You have built the calendar. You have called the wingman. You have started taking the mask off. You have walked through a hard week and picked up the closest piece. The book in your hands is one survivor's letter to another. One set of questions in the right order. One offer of a hand. The rest is in front of you.

I should have died. I didn't. If you have read this far, somewhere in the middle of all the questions, you also did not die. You are still here, and so am I. So is Terri, and so are the men and women whose names I will not put in this book. So is the next generation, the one you are part of, the one I am writing for. You don't get to choose your defining moment. You only get to choose what you do with the time that comes after it.

We are still here.

Now we live the tomorrows we almost lost.

Welcome home.

You don't get to choose your defining moment. You only get to choose what you do with the time that comes after it.

We are still here.

Now we live the tomorrows we almost lost.

Welcome home.

About the Author
Chris "Elroy" Stricklin

Eight-tenths of a second. That is the margin by which Chris "Elroy" Stricklin's story did not end on a desert airfield in Idaho on September 14, 2003. A United States Air Force Thunderbird Solo, flying Thunderbird Six at the "Gunfighter Skies" airshow at Mountain Home Air Force Base, he commanded the F-16 to the very edge of its envelope, rolled the jet away from the crowd, and ejected one hundred and forty feet above the ground, 0.8 seconds before impact one of the most photographed and documented ejections in aviation history. The aircraft was destroyed. The pilot walked away. He has spent every day since asking the question that frames the rest of his life, what do you owe the second chance you were never promised?

The answer, for Elroy, is what he calls a survivor's obligation, the responsibility to live with intention, lead with humility, and pour everything he learned in the cockpit back into the people and organizations he serves. It is the through-line connecting a small-town Alabama boyhood to the Pentagon, the White House, NATO command in Kabul, the founding presidency of a corporate university, and a national stage as an award-winning author and keynote speaker.

Selection to the U.S. Air Force Air Demonstration Squadron, the Thunderbirds, placed him among a handful of pilots in the world trusted to fly with show-line precision in front of millions. He flew the demanding Solo position. He felt, before most leaders ever do, what it is to operate where excellence and consequence share the same heartbeat then he lived the moment that would redefine excellence for him forever.

A Second Career Built on a Second Chance, he built a career on what the near-death experience taught him. He chose to put his name on the lesson then keep teaching it. After hanging up his uniform Elroy began to spend time with others, mentoring them on their journeys of leadership, healing and growth. This grew into an acclaimed keynote, Living an Intentional Life, which details his airshow ejection just 140 feet above the ground after a routine maneuver went unrecoverable. That decision, and the years that followed, became the foundation of his work helping leaders close the gap between what they planned for and what actually arrives then how to live a more intentional life.

The Man Behind the Mission is a combat-decorated fighter pilot, Chris holds degrees and certifications in Economics, Strategic Leadership, Financial Planning, Management, Real Estate, Strategic Studies, and Operational Art and Science. He has lived the rare combination he now teaches, the synthesis of speaking, following, leading, managing, negotiating, continuous improvement, and driving and positive change. But ask him to introduce himself and the credentials come last. He will tell you he is a husband to Terri, a father of four, and a son of Alabama who got eight-tenths of a second more than the math said he would, and who has been trying to be worth it ever since.

Live with intention.

Lead with humility.

Pay the second chance forward.

www.ingramcontent.com/pod-product-compliance
Lightning Source LLC
LaVergne TN
LVHW010840120826
845149LV00017B/3328
* 9 7 9 8 9 9 6 1 7 6 3 0 4 *